Fishing the Florida Keys

Fishing the Florida Keys

Wendell Endicott's
*Adventures with Rod and Harpoon
Along the Florida Keys*

Introduced and Edited by Paul Rich

WESTPHALIA PRESS
An imprint of the Policy Studies Organization

Fishing the Florida Keys
Wendell Endicott's
Adventures with Rod and Harpoon Along the Florida Keys

For information:
Westphalia Press
1527 New Hampshire Ave., N.W.
Washington, D.C. 20036

ISBN-13: 978-1935907190
ISBN-10: 1935907190

Updated material and comments on this edition can be found at the Westphalia Press website: westphaliapress.org

This edition is dedicated to
Robert Rich Jr., who like Wendell Endicott
is clearly a fisherman's fisherman.

THE FISHERMAN'S FISHERMAN

PREFACE TO NEW EDITION

WENDELL Endicott (1880-1954) was a great sportsman whose exploits included record-breaking adventures in the Florida Keys. Born in Massachusetts in 1880, he was a Harvard student from 1899 to 1901. He was an executive in the family business, the Endicott-Johnson Shoe Company and an investor in Sears, Roebuck. He was on the boards of directors of Chase Bank, R.H. Macy, and the First National Bank of Boston. He also was active in the Massachusetts Horticultural Society, the Metropolitan Opera Company, and the Boston Opera Company.

His real love was for the outdoors, burnishing a rod and reel. Described as "a fisherman's fisherman," his special avocation was for tarpon and the Florida

E

Keys. Generous with his time for those who wanted to learn the hobby, he liked to say he belonged to the fraternity of the Disciples of Izaak Walton.

In Dedham, outside Boston, he enlisted the famous New York architect Charles Platt to build a mansion with notable gardens, which on his death in 1954 was donated to MIT as a conference center. The center preserves a striking oil portrait of Wendell along with his trophies and sporting gear. Also on display throughout the house are the priceless paintings and Flemish tapestries that were part of his vision for the estate. This generosity has enabled many over the years to appreciate his enthusiasms.

Paul Rich

F

ADVENTURES
WITH ROD AND HARPOON
ALONG THE FLORIDA KEYS

"IT WAS IN ONE OF THESE CHANNELS THAT THE CAPTAIN
TOOK HIS RECORD TARPON OF 195 POUNDS"

ADVENTURES
WITH ROD AND HARPOON
ALONG THE FLORIDA KEYS

BY

WENDELL   ENDICOTT

*With eighty illustrations from photographs
by the author*

PREFACE

MANY a time have I been asked, "What luck did you have on your tarpon trip?" and always have I been able to reply, "Good luck."

Many a time have I listened to the unfortunate experiences of my friends or those of my friends' friends.

Probably every ardent fisherman at some time has had a great longing to experience the thrill of a contest with the "Silver King"—the most spectacular fighter of all the large game fish.

Thousands of sportsmen have made the attempt; hundreds have been disappointed, hundreds have been rewarded with a single adventure after days and nights of hard, conscientious work. A comparatively few have been able to "drink the cup of joy" to the full.

The southern waters abound in tarpon—but, alas, how successfully have they eluded the fisherman's lure.

Invariably have I questioned those disappointed friends, invariably has there seemed to me to be a reason for their failure: in other words, a perfectly natural ignorance as to time, place, and method.

I am far from posing as a Know-it-all, but my years of experience along the Florida Keys have, I believe, revealed some of the secrets that allow me to reply, "Good luck."

And by those words "Good luck" I happily include not only the successful adventures with the varied and interesting fish life in general, but the deep enjoyment, as well, of that "Enchanted Land."

There is much for me to learn—there are still new and rare adventures in store for me, of that I am sure; but still my recipe for "Good luck" has never failed me—and I would be happy to pass it on to the fraternity of "The Disciples of Izaak Walton."

W. E.

January, 1925.

CONTENTS

		PAGE
PREFACE		vii
CHAPTER		
I.	THE ENCHANTED LAND OF SPORT . . .	1
II.	A BAHIA HONDA FISH	12
III.	ADVENTURES WITH THE TARPON . . .	36
IV.	ACROBATS OF THE SEA	101
V.	ADVENTURES ON THE REEF	144
VI.	THE CAPRICIOUS BONEFISH	164
VII.	ADVENTURES WITH THE HARPOON . . .	183
VIII.	A GREAT AMERICAN MONUMENT . . .	226
IX.	FISHING FACTS AND SUGGESTIONS . . .	236

ILLUSTRATIONS

"It Was in One of These Channels That the Captain
   Took His Record Tarpon of 195 Pounds"   *Frontispiece*

PAGE

"I Wonder If in This Land of Enchantment—"   .   2
"That Marvel of Engineering Skill"   5
"Gliding in to Some Secluded Harbor"   .   .   .   9
" 'The Sonora,' Captain Walter Starck's Hospitable
   'Home' "   9
"Gazing Out on the Silent, Moonlit Waters"   .   .   10
An Evening at Bahia Honda   13
"The Angry Bulldog Shake of the Head!"   .   .   .   17
"Oh, the Power and Force of That Jump!"   .   .   21
"Back Into the Water Plunged the Fish"   .   .   .   22
"Then He Began a Series of Lesser Jumps"   .   .   25
"Another Mad Rush Answered That Question"   .   29
"The Shark Turned and Ran Out the Harpoon Line"   33
"Through the Many Beautiful Bays and Channels
   Winding in Among the Keys"   37
"There At the Mouth of the Creek You Will Find
   Your Crawfish"   41
"The Long Beach Looking Out Over the Atlantic
   and Shaded by Graceful and Artistic Cocoanut
   Palms"   45
"Having Had Explicit Instructions from My Daugh-
   ter to Bring Home 'Big Ones' "   49
"With Careful Fishing from a Rowboat"   .   .   .   53
Mr. Morgan Butler and His 154-Pound Tarpon   .   55

	PAGE
"The Cocoanut Palms of Long Key"	57
"Long Key Trestle Which Later in the Season Always Yields Many Good Fish"	61
Mrs. Henry Whitcomb and Her 135-Pound Tarpon	62
"One Has to Carry the Rowboats Over the Tracks"	67
"Knight's Key Trestle Is Next"	71
"There He Was, Rolling Limply from Side to Side"	77
"Fishing Sister Creek"	85
"One Begins His Fishing on Bahia Honda at the Trestles"	91
"An Evening's Catch at Bahia Honda" . . .	93
"Hink" and His 77-Pound Sailfish	99
"Up Into the Air Shot a Long Dark Fish" . . .	103
"Apparently Balancing Himself on the End of His Tail"	105
"This Time He Could Only Get His Head and Shoulders Out"	109
"Slowly and Carefully I Worked Him in Towards the Boat"	111
"He Lifted His Head Out of Water and Made One Last Effort to Throw the Hook"	113
"The Captain Reached Over the Side of the Boat and Grasped With Gloved Hand the Long Beak or Sword of the Fish"	117
"Several Times I Have Hooked Fish That Have Started Off With All Kinds of Jumps and Twists"	121
"There Was a Mad Rush to the Side" . . .	123
" 'Snappy Sport, I Calls It,' Says 'Hink,' As He Is Tossed Mountain High"	127
"Of Course Your First Thought Is to Watch for the Narrow Spike of His Tail Cutting the Surface of the Water"	129

PAGE

"How Fascinating It Is to See Those Straight, Lanky Fish Throw Themselves Slantwise Up Into the Air"　133

"Just Once in the Gulf Stream Have I Seen a Sunfish—But That Was Enough to Secure a Good Specimen" . . . .　135

"The Captain Had Lifted the Fish Against a Few Last Struggles" . . . .　139

"The Pelican—That Interesting, Wise Old Bird" .　145

"My Friend, John Haley, Who Has Brought in a 'Few Extra for Bill'" . . . . . .　146

"Then Again You May Glide Along by Some Trestle"　149

"A Sharp-Toothed Barracuda, the Tiger of the Sea"　151

"Looking Through Glass-Bottomed Pails You Gaze at Untold Beauty" . . . .　155

"You May Have Raised a Savage Barracuda" . .　157

"One of the Many Vessels That Are Constantly Plowing Along Toward the South" . . . . .　161

"His Shyness the Bonefish" . . . . . .　165

"You Stake Out Your Boat, Sit Down and Wait" .　169

"Six Bonefish Are the Most We Have Ever Taken on Any One Tide" . . . .　173

"One of the Most Favorable Banks Is That One Right Off Boot Key" . . . .　177

"We Built Sand Castles" . . . . . .　181

"We Gathered Shells" . . . .　181

"This Is No Child's Play" . . . . . .　185

"Picture, If You Can, Standing on the Bow of a Launch, Cruising Here and There Over the Shoals"　187

"One of These Vicious, Cruel and Repulsive Cannibals" . . . .　191

"A 'Close-Up' of a Cannibal" . . . . .　193

PAGE

"There I Saw a Jagged Hole Fully Ten Inches Long
and Four Inches Broad" 197
"And We in Turn Right Behind the Shark" . . 201
"It Took Considerable Tackle to Drag Him Up Onto
the Beach" 205
"Thus Were Five People With Arms Outstretched
Standing Crosswise on the Back of That Monster
Devil-Fish" 209
"My First Experience Was With the Heavy, Speedy
Whip-Ray" 211
"That Night I Was as Proud as Any Boy With My
First Two Trophies from the Harpoon" . . . 215
"Two Sawfish in Less Than Two Hours" . . . 217
"I Can See Those Little Groups of Barren Islands
Fairly Covered With Lazy Pelicans" . . . 221
"A Green Turtle" 223
"Strenuous It Was—But What a Morning!" . . 227
" 'Hink' in Action" 249
"I Claim That We Had the Right Kind of Bait,
Which Was Fresh" 259
"Casting That Heavy Net" 267
"It Requires, As a Matter of Fact, Considerable
Strength as Well as Skill to Throw Out Those
Umbrella-Like Nets" 269

[xiv]

"I WONDER IF IN THIS LAND OF ENCHANTMENT—"

ADVENTURES WITH ROD AND HARPOON

CHAPTER I

THE ENCHANTED LAND OF SPORT

TO see the "Silver King" leap high into the air in his efforts to free himself from hook and line; to watch the Gulf Stream acrobat, the sailfish, perform his antics; to feel the mad surface dash of the wahoo or the heavy downward pull of the amber-jack; to see and feel the lightning-like rush of the bone-fish—all these with almost endless contests with the multitudes of other kinds of fish, give to the lover of sport and "the out-of-doors" sensations and thrills that last long after he has left those fascinating little islands—the Keys of Florida—and returned to the busy whirl of city life and industry.

I wonder if in this land of enchantment the sunsets are not the most brilliant, the most glorious. I wonder also if there is any spot where the waters take on such varied and marvelous colors.

I can picture now the absorbing beauty of the melting of day into night. Not even the expectant strike of a tarpon as one glides silently along the trestles or over some deep channel, deters one from absorbing that beauty of sky and sea.

There are many times when one is thoroughly content to lean back in comfort—open one's arms to the gentle breeze and feast one's eyes and satisfy one's soul with nature's ever changing, ever fascinating wonderment of glory.

There in the waters you see a golden yellow, edged by a pale light green; here you see the colors of a topaz; there you see the shadings of an emerald; here an olive green; there a Nile green—and out beyond is the deep liquid blue. A cloud drifts over the sun and the colors change; the sun shines forth again and you see new combinations—new colors—new glories. And then when finally the sun.sets silently behind a distant key, those broad expanses of

No. 5 Trestle

Knight's Key Trestle

Bahia Honda Trestle

"THAT MARVEL OF ENGINEERING SKILL"

—*Page* 8

[5]

calm shallow waters reflect that brilliance of sunset glow—those soft indescribable pinks, deepening, ever changing, to flame and carmine.

One evening, I remember it so well, the sun had set a disc of flame behind a thin gray mist which in itself took on a flame-like glow. The clouds above, shaped like long banners radiating from the glowing horizon, drew up in their folds those sunset colors and in turn were mirrored in the glass-like surface of Bahia Honda. As if by magic, the surface became alive with rolling tarpon: hundreds—yes, thousands—broke the surface of the bay and splashed the waters with the final quick flip of their tail. The sky—the water—the fish—sent thrills of wonder at nature's glorious display. I have heard that evening referred to by an old fishing captain who was there: "The whole darned place just boiled with acres of 'em." It is only fair to say that my peace of mind was soon upset by one of the grandest fights I ever had with a tarpon—but more of that anon.

This is the land of the Florida Keys—islands, large and small, grouped and spotted at intervals from the southern reaches of the Florida mainland to Key West, the jumping-off place to Cuba. The water itself is singularly shallow with bars and shoals—channels and bays—making it ideal with its many protected and attractive harbors for boats of shallow draft.

Over many of these islands and across many of these channels and bays stretches that marvel of engineering skill, the Florida East Coast Railroad. One fairly gasps at the courage of the man, Henry M. Flagler, who had the conception, the determination and the power to push through to completion a work of such magnitude. And yet how often is Mr. Flagler or his railroad company "cussed" when some wise tarpon, finding himself hooked, decides to take a turn or two around a trestle, or seeks the friendly company of an old sunken construction pile.

But then again, how often is the Flagler system blessed when one of the trains brings to the sportsman a fresh supply of water, of ice, of food—to say nothing of letters from home.

Gliding into some secluded harbor within a

"GLIDING INTO SOME SECLUDED HARBOR"

" 'THE SONORA,' CAPTAIN WALTER STARCK'S HOSPITABLE 'HOME' "

—Page 8

[9]

"GAZING OUT ON THE SILENT, MOONLIT WATERS"

—*Page* 11

stone's throw of the best fishing grounds in the world—free to try one's skill in the great variety of sport with rod or harpoon—free to wander on the coral beaches or rest under the overhanging cocoanut palms—free to enjoy a quiet evening's smoke, gazing out on the silent, moonlit waters, silent save for the splash of some feeding fish or the cry of some nocturnal bird—a new and wonderful world of sport and beauty is indeed offered to him who has entered that enchanted land.

And who in describing the silent and active joys of that southern life could fail to mention the delicious luxury of the morning bath on deck. Standing there in nature's garb, dried by the early sun and gentle breeze, stayed perhaps by a sip of coffee, a breakfast appetizer, one indeed is eager for the day, eager for some new adventure of sport, some new feast of nature's beauty.

CHAPTER II

A BAHIA HONDA FISH

THE story of the tarpon has been told by many writers and fishermen. As a rule each one has a little something new to say, each one has learned something different, each one has discovered some novel trait. And why not? Because the "Silver King" is indeed a fish of many surprises. No one knows that truth better than the man who has followed that exhilarating sport for many seasons—bringing to the boat's side large fish and small fish, long ones and short ones, thick ones and thin ones, in different depths of waters, in different currents of tides, in cool and warm weather, on windy and calm days or nights— each fish under each condition giving almost without exception some new experience, some new thrill.

Every fisherman has the same trait, born from his enthusiasm of the sport, to tell the story of how he caught his big fish—of how he lost his

AN EVENING AT BAHIA HONDA

Captain Butler Roberts, John K. Howard and Joseph B. Russell, Jr.

record fish. He is patient as a listener, just so
that when his turn comes around he can begin
with "now that reminds me of the time"; and
so I am a common fisherman with the rest and
I begin my tales of sport hoping that I too
may have found some new angle for him who
has already had some experience, or may be
of some help to the novice who would wish to
enter that enchanted land of sport and beauty
around the Florida Keys and join the ranks of
East Coast fishermen.

The day had been rather hot and we waited
for the sun to get well down before we put out
in our launch for the trestles of Bahia Honda.
I took the wheel while the Captain put the
final touches to the bait. As usual, there was
the restless expectancy, the usual expressions of
opinion, the usual expounding of fish lore and
logic. Although our little harbor where we
lay at Bahia Honda is only fifteen or twenty
minutes from the trestle, it always seems to me
a long trip taking twice the time. I wonder
if every enthusiastic fisherman, while gifted
with boundless patience when the rod is once in
his hand, is not always a bit impatient until

he finally has reached "the place to begin" and has cast his line overboard. Long before he reaches that spot, he has his fishing belt adjusted, his rod in hand, and he at least is ready.

On this afternoon, I was no exception. I had taken this same trip many times before, had landed and released many of those noble fish from under those trestles, but still there was that "something new" to expect, something different to meet and negotiate.

In really quick time we were down by the trestles. The ebb-tide was not too heavy and conditions looked good. We swung into the usual spot—the fifth arch to the eastward from the central arch—and with about ninety feet of line we let the bait drift down with the tide, working it slowly from below the arch to above the arch, up and down between the piers.

There was a sharp strike and I was ready on the instant. It proved to be only a "Jack," but I mention this as I have found that many good tarpon are lost by fishermen not playing every strike for a tarpon—thereby giving careless slack or failing properly to set the hook. It was under this very arch a year before that

"THE ANGRY BULLDOG SHAKE OF THE HEAD!"

—*Page* 23

my good companion, Joseph Russell, Jr., raised
and landed the largest tarpon I have ever seen
brought to gaff, weighing 187 pounds. This
weight was taken after the fish had been out of
the water over twenty-four hours, so at the time
the fish was landed, I have always felt a conservative estimate would be 191 pounds.

In this way, we worked Arch Number Four,
Number Three, Number Two, and so on,
covering it back again, but all without result.
My constant friend and fishing companion,
Harold Keith, was getting nervous for a change
of bait, so he shifted to a whole mullet. Still
no results and I switched to a spoon. It is only
on rare occasions that a spoon will raise a fish
but still I have seen it work when no other
lure would create interest. In fact my "first"
tarpon was taken on a spoon. Suddenly our
ever watchful captain sang out, "There they
are!" and we turned just in time to see a group
of foamy splashes about four hundred yards
out in the bay. We speeded up the launch,
changed back to the old reliable "cut bait" and
steered for the school of fish. The fish were
headed out into the middle of the bay and were

moving fast. Another party fishing some distance away had seen the fish and they too put on speed and headed after the school.

Then came the interesting exhibition of watching the two captains try to manipulate the launches so as to get in a favorable position above the school. Of course each captain showed the other due consideration, but still each was ready to take advantage of any tactical error. At last we thought we were just right and with every muscle tense ready for the thrill of a heavy strike, we waited. The neighboring launch was now close to us and every one was all expectancy—all ready to give that "tarpon yell" that proclaims to all within a mile that "a tarpon is in the air." But just about that time some nervous chap beside us conceived the idea that the tip and butt of his rod were not tight enough and hastened to pound the butt of his rod on the bottom of the boat. Good-by, tarpon. They put for the bottom and the surface of Bahia Honda was mirror-like in its placid peacefulness.

The Captain is mild in speech, but I have every reason to believe his thoughts concurred

"OH, THE POWER AND FORCE OF THAT JUMP!"

—*Page* 23

[21]

"BACK INTO THE WATER PLUNGED THE FISH"

—Page 24

entirely with what I said. However, that was "ancient history," and off we put again to the trestles.

It was just at this time that the sun set in all its glory and the skies and waters were illuminated like the glow of embers. And it was just at this time that we saw the "acres of tarpon" —a sight never to be forgotten.

Suddenly I felt the heavy solid strike and I as suddenly struck back. Then came the quick out-take of line. The Captain, always on his toes, was ready at the throttle. The launch jumped forward to take up any possible slack, and up out of the water shot a long, heavy, silver, gleaming monster. Oh, the power and force of that jump!—the angry bulldog shake of the head! Was the hook well set or would he throw it out? I waited in suspense, fearing to see the hook go spinning through the air and to feel that sickening slack. Here indeed was a fish worth fighting for, here was a big fellow —and just as if I had never taken a fish before —just as if the Captain were watching his first contest—just as if Keith had the fish on his own line—the three of us burst forth in such "tarpon yells" as might easily have shaken the foundations of the piers themselves. Back into the water plunged the fish, and in an instant up again higher than before. It seemed to me as if he cleared the surface by at least eight feet. Hardly had he touched the water when he began a series of three lesser jumps. Then came the mad rush.

"Look out!" the Captain shouted. "He's headed for the trestles!"

"Hold him!" joined in my companion. But even in the excitement of the rush I could hear Keith chuckle at the utter futility of this bit of advice.

"Hold nothing!" I shouted. "Watch out, Captain, he's gone through!"

And at that instant, with the trestle between us, he made another superb jump into the air, followed by a rush to the side. On the instant, I threw off my drag, because one rub of that taut line on the concrete pier would have cut my tackle like the stroke of a sharp knife.

The Captain, watching each maneuver of the fish, had turned the boat and was headed through the arch. Then came quick work at

"THEN HE BEGAN A SERIES OF LESSER JUMPS"

—*Page* 24

reeling in the slack as we shot into the tide under the trestle. We held our breath. Was he still on? A tightening of the line and another mad rush answered that question.

"Pull him in," advised Keith with another chuckle; "I want to do a little fishing myself."

But by this time the humor of the situation was lacking and I was hard at work "pumping," trying to make some impression on that fighting monster on the other end of my line. But realizing I had considerable of a task ahead of me and having had experience with big tarpon and knowing what I was in for, I settled back with the full determination to let my fish do most of the work and fight him only when I felt any slight easing up on his part.

Suddenly a new note was sounded in the battle. The Captain, with eyes in every direction, caught a distant shadow in the water. "A shark, and a big one too!"

Slowly and ominously that shadow moved toward the spot where my fish was fighting. The cry of shark to the fisherman sends a chill of horror, fright and anger to his very soul. Here indeed is the "devil" of the southern waters. Here indeed is a cannibal who is always cruising around just waiting for some one or something to get into trouble and then to appear on the scene—to kill and destroy. He has little or no chance of catching his prey when that prey is sound and healthy, but let that prey be wounded or in trouble and you will find a shark close at hand to rush and destroy with ferocious cruelty and determination.

This time the words came with all earnestness. "Pull him in, Mr. Endicott, or you'll lose him!" urged the Captain. Ah, how easy it was to give this advice, but how difficult was my work!

There was no time to lose. Pump I did, with every bit of energy I had in me. Both I and the tackle were strained to the limit. I would gain a few yards and then Mr. Tarpon would make a rush and not only take out those few gained yards but a few more as well for good measure. The strain was telling on us both, but fortunately I began to make some headway.

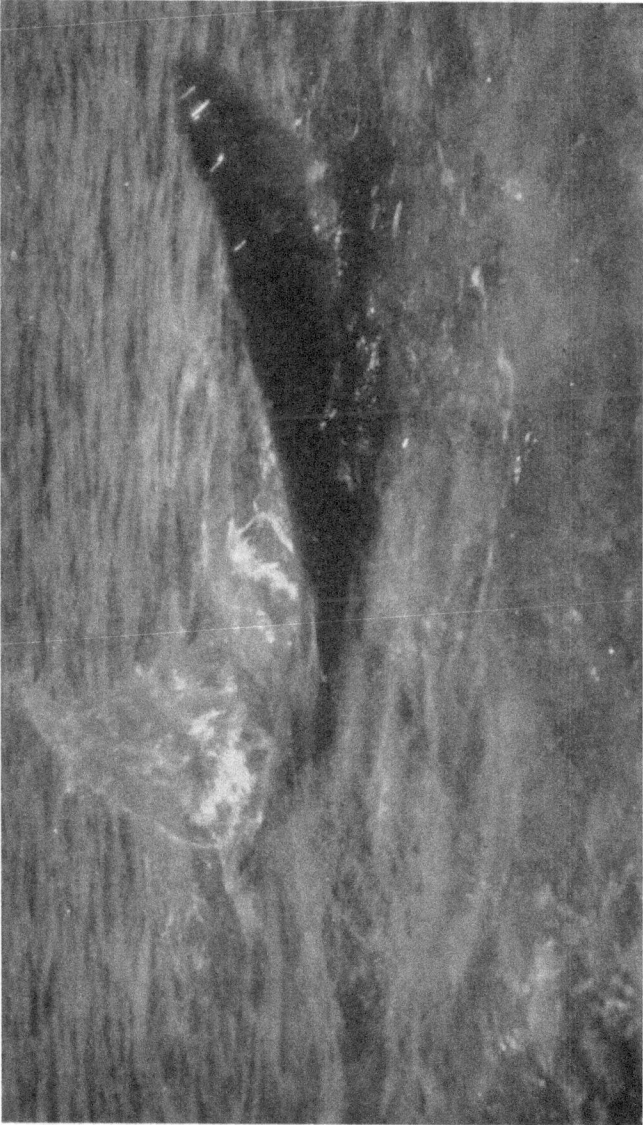

"ANOTHER MAD RUSH ANSWERED THAT QUESTION"

—*Page 27*

All this time the shadow was getting closer and closer.

"He's after him!" shouted the Captain.

There was another rush and then a sudden stop. My heart sank; but knowing that oftentimes a tarpon gives up his fight when attacked by a shark, I began to pump and reel with the last few ounces of strength I had left. The weight was still there and my only hope was that there was a whole fish on the end of the line instead of half a fish.

"Quick!" shouted the Captain. "Keep him coming!"

I gritted my teeth and bent a little harder to my job.

"Quicker!" shouted the Captain again. "The shark is close behind!"

Even then I could see the shark sheering off and darting forward for another attack. I made one last mighty heave and the shark made one last mighty rush; but in his determination to seize his prey in those pitiless jaws, he came within range and the Captain, standing on the very edge of the stern, threw the harpoon and buried that arrow-like dart deep into the side of that monster cannibal.

"Now what?" said the Captain quietly, with a smile of satisfaction as the shark turned and ran out the harpoon line.

"We want them both," was my answer.

But that was not to be. The tarpon, evidently with a keen eye for the "main chance," made up his mind that there was still freedom to be gained, and with renewed vigor he put off with equal speed in the opposite direction. "Now, what indeed?" I said. A lost tarpon or a lost harpoon? And I elected to save the fish.

The Captain, however, put in every bit of his strength to check the rush of the shark and even risked the burning of his hands, but all to no purpose. The end of the harpoon line was in sight and there was no buoy attached. The Captain made a hasty turn around the cleat, but the shark never stopped. There was a snap and the line parted, and as far as I know the shark is going still.

"Well," said the Captain, "now let's get the tarpon." But the renewed strength of the fish was now visited upon the fisherman and I shall

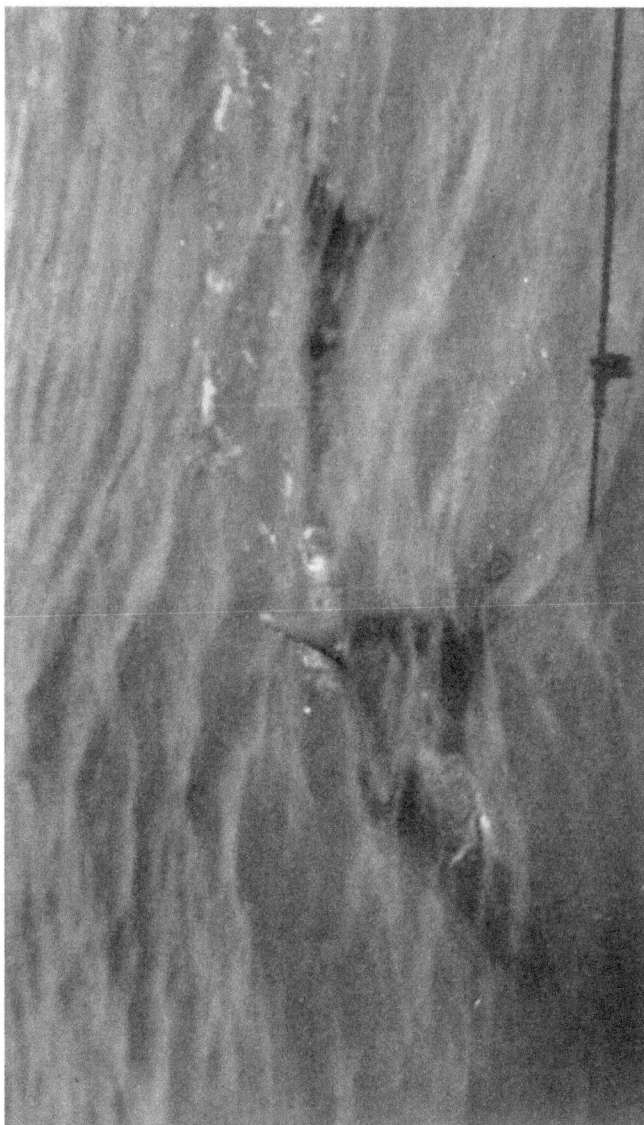

"THE SHARK TURNED AND RAN OUT THE HARPOON LINE"

—*Page* 32

have to admit that my efforts by that time were feeble and ineffective, and so the fight continued; but at last I won and at the end of one hour and forty minutes I brought to the boat a splendid fish of 165 pounds.

CHAPTER III

ADVENTURES WITH THE TARPON

THE usual approach to the haunts of the tarpon is from the north. One starting from Miami cannot fail to enjoy the trip down through the many beautiful bays and channels winding in among the Keys. Sometimes you will head for Ragged Key where there is a delightful little harbor, and perhaps you will have time to slip out and catch a few grunts in the south channel. I question if there is anything more delicious for breakfast than a fresh-caught grunt.

Sometimes you will head for Angel Fish Creek and while you are there perhaps your mouth will water for a cold crawfish salad, which when properly prepared is one of the greatest delicacies the country has to offer. I have yet to see any one who did not admit its superiority to the lobster. One of my first duties when reaching Angel Fish Creek is to

"THROUGH THE MANY BEAUTIFUL BAYS AND CHANNELS
WINDING IN AMONG THE KEYS"

—*Page* 36

slip into a launch, head through the creek toward the ocean, take the right-hand turn, and there at the mouth of the creek to find our crawfish. Incidentally, it is wise to have an extra supply of these crawfish, which I have found to be the best bait for bottom fishing. Fresh crawfish, when available, is preferable for bait; but it is also wise, when crawfish are plentiful, to salt down a few for emergency.

Here, too, one takes his first sally out into "the blue" of the Gulf Stream for sailfish or onto the reefs for the amber-jack, the barracuda, the grouper, the kingfish and other "reef fish."

Perhaps one will stop in Barnes Sound for the night, and if he looks carefully he may get his first view of a tarpon rolling. He may even "give it a try," and especially along the western shore he will have a good chance of "jumping a fish."

Sometimes he will head direct for Tavernier. Personally, I am always a little impatient until we reach this spot. This little harbor has indeed yielded many hours of rare good sport.

I remember one night we were fishing for mangrove snappers in the creek right near the one-arch bridge and my little six-year-old daughter was having quite a struggle trying to handle these strong-pulling fish. Suddenly several small silvery fish broke water just where she was fishing.

"Baby tarpon," said the Captain.

"Good," said I; "let's go back to the boat."

I wanted to try an experiment, and soon I was out in the rowboat with my six-ounce trout rod rigged up and a small strip of balao for bait. The fish took well and I had as sporty a few hours' fishing as I ever experienced. With the heavy tide running and with the rather large bait for that light rod, it was hard to hook those little fish. They would strike and make a glorious leap of six or eight feet into the air and, like their great-grandfathers, shake their heads and throw the hook. I found, however, that by holding the rod straight back and striking with the line only and then giving them the play of the limber rod, I was quite successful. And how they did run and jump—up into the air, up-stream, down-stream—in fact, "all over the lot." They were lightly hooked and easily freed, so no harm was done,

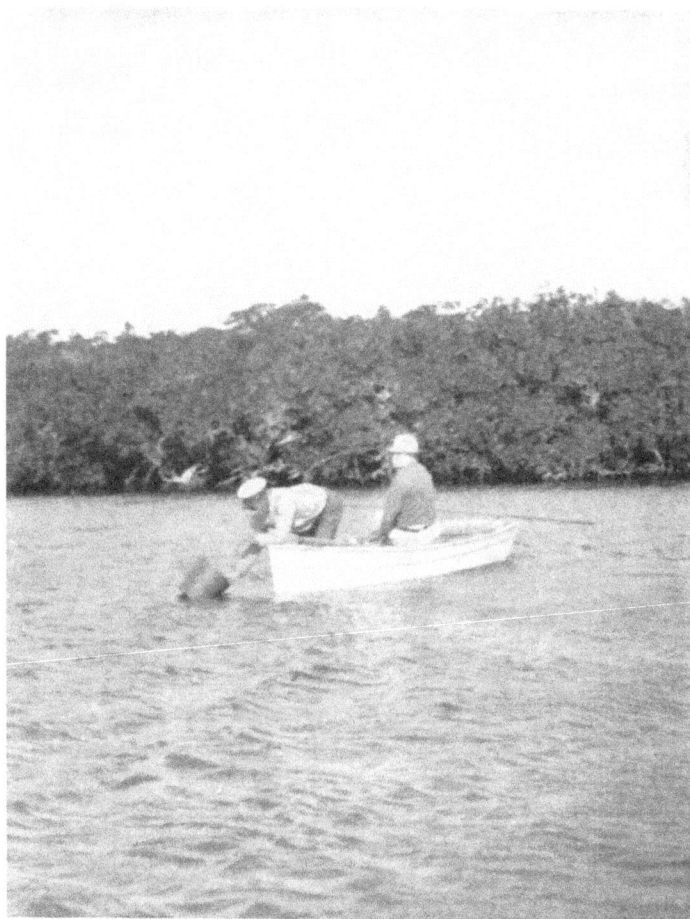

"THERE AT THE MOUTH OF THE CREEK YOU WILL FIND
YOUR CRAWFISH"

—*Page* 39

[41]

but it certainly was exhilarating sport with that light tackle.

It is from this point, also, that one seriously starts out for the sailfish. And not far from there is to my mind the best of all the bonefish banks, just off Rodriguez Key—but more of that later.

The next harbor to make for and the first real station for the tarpon is Trestle No. 2. Somehow to me this is the most charming of all the harbors. There you anchor under the shadow of South Matacumbe—a beautiful key covered with that glossy green mangrove bush and edged with attractive and clean little beaches. To the west you look over a broad shoal across the bay to Long Key beyond and the broad shoal waters of the Bay of Florida dotted with many other small keys. Just over the embankment to the southeast is the long beach looking out over the Atlantic and shaded by the graceful and artistic cocoanut palms. Many is the delightful stroll I have had along that beach and many are the beautiful shells that my little daughter has picked up there and brought back to the boat with as much pride and joy as her daddy ever had in bringing back some large species of the finny tribe.

It is from this beautiful little harbor that we start on our real serious crusade with rod and harpoon—or drink in with the most profound wonder the glories of color in sky and water.

From this point one fishes Lignum Vitæ Channel, Trestle No. 2, and Trestle No. 5. Personally I have always had more luck at jumping fish at the westward end of Trestle No. 5 on the ebb-tide. It is very hard to fish the flood-tide at that spot on account of the dangerous and sunken old construction piles on the ocean side of the trestle. The channels extending out into the bay at times yield even more fish than the trestles themselves. It was in one of these channels that the Captain took his record tarpon of 195 pounds.

I had a very interesting demonstration at Trestle No. 5 one night, bearing out my contention that whenever possible one should fish for tarpon from a rowboat rather than from a launch. It is my belief that the tarpon is very sensitive to noise in the water and that the churn of the propeller and the throb and pound of the

"THE LONG BEACH LOOKING OUT OVER THE ATLANTIC AND SHADED BY GRACEFUL AND ARTISTIC COCOANUT PALMS"

—*Page 43*

[45]

engine have ruined many a good evening's sport, especially in shoal waters. I have found that the boat itself or the quiet movement of the oars has but little effect on the fish.

This particular evening in question we had taken up our position in a rowboat at Trestle No. 5 and just at that time a party in a launch swung into the trestle just below us. We lost thereby what we considered to be the best position—best from experience and best because we had just seen fish rolling there. Knowing that there was little use to work back toward the launch, we kept well up along the arches. They on their part, knowing they had the best position, did not disturb us. That night the fish were striking very "light." One could never tell but that the light touches were small fish of some sort, but experience had taught me to play everything for a tarpon, and soon I had one of the silvery monsters in the air. Perhaps there was a little more than the usual emphasis thrown into the "tarpon yell" for the benefit of our neighbors in the launch. We certainly gave our lungs good exercise as well as our bodies. How the Captain did lay back on the oars and how that fish did jump and fight! At times it seemed as if we were a cockle-shell being blown about at will, but it was thrilling and exciting. Helping to steer the boat by the position in which I held the rod, and taking every advantage that the fish gave us, the Captain finally worked the boat to a nearby shoal, leaned back with a grunt of relief and advised me in a friendly way to "go to it." The fish was not as anxious to reach the shoal as we were, nor was he willing to yield to my attempted persuasions, but on the other hand he gave me a fine exhibition—running off all my well-gained line and ending with several superb jumps in the air. That brought forth more exuberant "yells"—which was perhaps not kind.

In due time he was brought to gaff, and being my first big fish of the season and having had explicit instructions from my daughter to bring home some "big ones" we took him aboard. He was indeed a handsome fish of 135 pounds.

Soon we were at it again with the same relative positions at the trestle. We took two more fish and jumped a fourth while our neighbors in the launch fished with no results whatsoever.

"HAVING HAD EXPLICIT INSTRUCTIONS FROM MY
DAUGHTER TO BRING HOME 'BIG ONES'"

—*Page* 48

[49]

Now I do not mean to infer that a launch is hopeless at a trestle, because I have taken many fish myself from a launch, but I do believe that I have fished many empty evenings from a launch when, if I could have used a rowboat, I would have been rewarded.

Speaking on this point, there is one particular spot, Grouper Channel, that the Captain and I have studied with great care. The channel that the fish frequent is narrow and comparatively shallow. It is quite easy from a launch to jump one or two fish but, with rare exceptions, that ends it as far as the big fish go.

After a few "turns" you see the school of big fish rolling well out from the trestle and headed toward the ocean. Curiously enough, it may be twenty-four or forty-eight hours before they come back again. On the other hand, with careful fishing from a rowboat I have from that small inconspicuous spot taken as high as five good fish and in addition lost several others who freed themselves in some glorious spectacular jumps.

From Trestles No. 2 and No. 5 one's next move is to Tom's Harbor—an excellent anchorage ground but quite hard to navigate. Tom's Harbor is but a short distance from Long Key and is just the other side of Long Key Trestle.

For those who are unable to make the fishing trip by yacht or house-boat, the Long Key Fishing Camps, operated by the Florida East Coast Railway and situated most delightfully among the cocoanut palms, offer comfortable and attractive accommodations to the fisherman. It was from these camps that Mr. Zane Grey wrote many of his delightful tales of fishing. The camps, as a rule, close soon after the time the best of the tarpon season begins, although our party have taken as high as sixty-five tarpon in March. On the other hand, the best fishing we ever had was during a six-day trip at the end of May. Our party of four, fishing from two boats, took fifty-three tarpon in those six days. We had the satisfaction of releasing fifty out of the fifty-three fish taken. The total estimated weight was 4,920 pounds. The average weight per fish was 92.8 pounds. This included two baby tarpon weighing 7 pounds each. Included in this record it is interesting to note

"WITH CAREFUL FISHING FROM A ROWBOAT"

—*Page* 51

MR. MORGAN BUTLER AND HIS 154-POUND TARPON

Captain Starck landing the fish

"THE COCOANUT PALMS OF LONG KEY"

—*Page* 52

the following large fish which we estimated as follows: 185-175-160-160-154 (actual weight)-140. I say "estimated weight" as it must necessarily be an estimate on released fish. I have no hesitancy, however, in quoting these figures as I have faith in the Captain's almost accurate judgment in estimating weights. On almost every fish I have ever taken and weighed I have found that the Captain was too conservative.

The Long Key Fishing Camps are, however, open throughout the height of the sailfish season.

Visitors are always welcome to these camps and it is well worth while stopping off to see in the main hall the really splendid collection of local fish mounted attractively and hung on the walls. Note particularly the "head and shoulders" of a tarpon. This part of the fish, weighing one hundred and fifty-three pounds, was all that was landed; a cannibal shark had destroyed what would have been without doubt the record tarpon of all time. Scientific measurements indicated that the fish would have weighed well over two hundred pounds.

From Tom's Harbor one fishes the two best places on the west end of the Long Key Trestle which late in the season always yield many good fish. We had an excellent illustration at this trestle one morning of the damage a launch can do to a shoal fishing ground.

We arrived early so as to get the fish at the first of the ebb as they worked out from the trestle into the narrow channel leading toward the west. The channel was full of big fish and we were all ready to slip out in the rowboats. Just at that time another boat dropped anchor right in this chosen spot. Out they piled in a noisy launch right down through the channel to the trestle. In a few minutes, instead of seeing lazily rolling fish, we saw two large schools well broken up going at express-train speed out into the distant bay. Hoping that the launch would have created less disturbance in the deeper water near the trestle, we rowed down there. "No fish here," they said, as they "chug-chugged" by us. Back they went into the channel, kicking up the same noisy fuss. In about half an hour after they left the trestle, I did jump one fish, but that was all. In about an-

"LONG KEY TRESTLE WHICH LATER IN THE SEASON
ALWAYS YIELDS MANY GOOD FISH"

Mr. Morgan Butler and his 154-pound tarpon

—Page 60

[61]

MRS. HENRY WHITCOMB AND HER 135-POUND TARPON

other half-hour they had pulled up and departed. We tried the channels, but all to no purpose. The fish had left. What was the result? They had no fish, we had no fish, and our morning's sport was ruined.

It was only two days before that we had fished that same place in a rowboat. The fish were there; we took three—one fish my record of 185 pounds, one 154 pounds, and one 70 pounds—and when we stopped the tarpon were still rolling lazily in that narrow shallow channel just where we had been fishing. Whereas on the morning of the invasion of the launch they got nothing and we got nothing. If everybody had used rowboats there is not the slightest question but what we all would have jumped fish.

The two Tom's Harbor Trestles just beyond are almost always good for fish of smaller size. One of my most enjoyable experiences in tarpon fishing was at Tom's Harbor Trestle.

It was early in March, but the several days of light easterly winds had warmed up the waters to such a degree that we were easily tempted to forget our sailfishing off Trestle No.

2 and head for Tom's Harbor. Besides, the barometer had dropped considerably, which indicated a change of weather with colder winds from the west or north. It is just on such a change as that that one wants to be "on the ground" and ready for a "big night." The moon was up, but fortunately the sky was well clouded. It has always seemed strange to me that on clear moonlight nights the fishing is almost invariably poor while on nights that are "as black as your pocket" the fish will strike well. I have had that demonstrated many times and even demonstrated in one evening. For instance, I have been out fishing with constant strikes in the dark of the evening until the moon came up, when all activities ceased.

This evening the sky was well clouded. There was not a breath of wind and as we approached the trestles we could hear the tarpon making savage lunges, followed by the skip, skip, skip of a frightened balao as he made his escape for life. The tarpon that night were making no lazy rolls but were striking and lunging with all the savageness of a barracuda.

Hardly had I put overboard and before I could set my drags and strike against the slack line I was letting out, there was a tug—a rush—a jump—a big splash—and a snarl of slack line around my feet followed by a muttered comment. The next time I was ready, soon finding out that forty or fifty feet of line was all that was necessary.

Knowing that the fish for the most part run small, I was prepared with my light tackle, which added tremendously to the contests. That night I landed and freed ten tarpon, which was my record number for any one evening's fishing. As expected, they were not large fish—the largest weighing about fifty pounds. But all being taken on light tackle gave most excellent sport. I had jumped and lost five other fish. To a salmon fisherman that sounds like careless or ignorant execution but in tarpon fishing I should consider it well above the average, even of the most experienced. On the other hand, I have seen my good friend, Herbert Straus, on his first tarpon trip take a total of fifteen fish in ten days' fishing and lose only three. It was somehow curious that he never agreed with me when I began to expound on the question of luck.

What would have happened to us that night if the wind hadn't changed and a sudden storm rolled up to stop us and drive us back to the boat will always remain one of "the fisherman's guesses."

There was one little incident that night that I should like to mention in illustrating the sensitiveness and wariness of the tarpon. Just as we were in the midst of lively action some rowboat out looking for bait came through the trestle, possibly three hundred yards away and went out onto the shoals perhaps four or five hundred yards distant. On the bow of this boat was a gasolene lamp in full glow. The light was of course very apparent to us and for fully ten minutes until the light disappeared there wasn't a strike nor a movement of any fish as far as we could see, or hear, or feel.

The next "port" below is Key Vaca Channel. One makes one's way almost up to the railroad track and anchors in a deep but secluded little harbor. At this point the railroad embankment-

"ONE HAS TO CARRY THE ROWBOATS OVER THE TRACKS"

—*Page* 69

fill is carried across the channel so there is no connection with the fishing grounds on the outer side. One has to carry the rowboats over the tracks and launch them on the ocean side.

The character of fishing in the Key Vaca Channel is somewhat different from the fishing at the trestles. Here one does not have the swift tides to consider nor the danger of the trestles themselves nor any old construction work. Here it is open and clear and one is given great leeway in which to fight his fish. So without the handicap of tide and trestles, one can with reasonable care use his light tackle. The tarpon on his part, not having the drag of heavier line and tide, has more freedom in his play. Here we use to good advantage the live mullet for bait and troll slowly over the grounds. This is extremely interesting fishing, for oftentimes before the tarpon strikes you feel the live bait begin to pull and struggle. You know then that the big fish are around. Suddenly you see the mullet jump out of the water and at that instant there is a huge lunge and splash. The tarpon has made a strike and failed to get the bait. But if he is anxious he'll follow it up and then the fun begins. In using the live mullet one must be careful not to strike the fish at once but rather allow him to run a few feet, giving him time to get the bait well into his mouth. Free and uncontrolled as the fish is, he makes the highest and most glorious leaps into the air. I have seen the tarpon, and they are invariably big fish at Key Vaca, clear the water by fully eight or ten feet—not once but many times. At no place I have ever fished have I seen such spectacular leaps, and all this on light tackle and a clear field allows one to enjoy the fight to the last degree.

Key Vaca yielded to us one evening eight fish of the following estimated weights: 175-161-160-135-120-110-90-70. I say "estimated weights" as we fortunately were able to release them all. That evening the fish struck heavily and constantly until the phosphorescence appeared very prominently, when all activities ceased.

Here again the rowboat proves its superiority to the launch. I have known the launch, after one has landed a fish or two, to frighten all the

—Page 73

"KNIGHT'S KEY TRESTLE IS NEXT"

tarpon out of the channel and thereby ruin the fishing for at least twenty-four hours. It is only fair to say, however, in this connection, that it is tremendously hard work for the man at the oars and while the captains have unusual endurance and invariably approach the work with willingness and enthusiasm, much can be done on the part of the fisherman in his consideration of time and conditions. In other words, it is the "choice" way of fishing but should be used with fair and reasonable discretion.

Knight's Key is next. Ah, the memories connected with that trestle—that old sunken pier extending out toward the ocean! It is the ground of my first endeavors. The place where I saw a tarpon for the first time "in the air." Saw, but not landed! And here is a story of great fortitude.

Keith and I were together. It was our first night out and we were as excited as two school boys in search of adventure. I can see us now, stiff, tense and awkward, asking questions, trying to absorb instructions as to what to do and when to do it, ignorant entirely of what was in store for us. Being more of an experienced fisherman, I was perhaps a little patronizing; but how really ignorant I was! I had landed amber-jacks, grouper and barracuda before and thought I knew the sensation of a tarpon fight; but, alas, I didn't.

That night the fish hit hard—the Captain started the launch—there was a mad take-out of the line—a jump—a splash—and a few handfuls of slack. "What happened? What did I do wrong? Was it my fault?" and countless other questions were flung at a quietly smiling captain. Of course my heart sank. I felt I had disgraced myself and the boat. The fish that I had been waiting for for years had given me the opportunity and I had failed. I was feeling pretty low and rather sorry for myself when there was a bang, a rush and a yell from Keith. He had hooked a fish. It jumped and it stayed on. My feeling of failure disappeared in the excitement of my friend's contest and my first view of a tarpon fight. As I think of it now, I marvel at any man being able to take the hundreds of directions that were flung at him: excited ones by me; calm, intelligent ones by the Captain. Undoubtedly, however, he neither heard nor understood. In reality, to use a slang expression, the monster fish "just played horse with him" as every big tarpon does with every beginner.

Somehow we got away from the trestles and turned on the searchlight to watch the fight. I shall never forget my first view of a mass of gleaming silver shooting up into the light out of that black mysterious water; I shall never forget the shake of his head, the twist in the air, and the mighty splash. And fight they did. I could see Keith putting every last bit of strength he had in him into the rod and into the pumping. Here was his first fish and a big one too and he was going to get him if he died for it. As the light flickered across his face, I could see that he actually turned white, that there were big beads of perspiration standing out on his forehead, and that he was all a-tremble. "Wendell," I heard him mutter, "I wonder if I can hold out." The seconds went into minutes and the minutes into an hour and still the fight kept on.

By that time all was still except an occasional word of encouragement from the Captain. As

for me, I was suffering with my companion—
suffering with anxiety, thrilled with excitement.
Could he indeed last? Could he ever bring that
fish to gaff? The Captain was ready. I was
in a daze and the man with the rod was
ready to "pass out." At last there he was,
rolling limply from side to side, a silvery streak
just under the surface of the water, his eyes
like two gleaming balls of fire. Nearer and
nearer he was "pumped" toward the boat.
"Pump him again," said the Captain; but the
tarpon moved slowly. There he was, almost
within reach of the gaff—a prize worthy of any
man's endeavor. But—and how often there is
a "but"—the tarpon limply swung on his other
side and the hook came out. He lay there for
a moment, flipped his tail; then slowly headed
back into those mysterious depths.

A deathly silence came over us—words failed
me.

"Well," said Keith, "it was a good fight."

He said no more. That is what I call fortitude. It was considerably over an hour of
grueling work and the keenest kind of disap-

"THERE HE WAS, ROLLING LIMPLY FROM SIDE TO SIDE"

—Page 76

pointment. He laughs at it to-day but it was no laughing matter then.

One might say that the best place to fish at the Knight's Key Trestle starts at about the tenth span from the eastward end and extends as far as the thirty-fourth span. Small tarpon, however, can often be taken right from the first span. On the concrete pier at the thirty-fourth arch is a large white paint spot. This marks the sunken piles of the old wharf that extends out perhaps three hundred yards toward the ocean. The best spots to fish are close to those piles with the preference of an ebb-tide. It is very hard and dangerous to negotiate this fishing ground in a launch, especially in the night, but from a rowboat one can get into the very heart of the best places. There is always, however, the danger of fouling the fish on the piles and many good fish have been lost in just that way. Nevertheless, it is one of the surest places to jump tarpon on the East Coast.

If one were to ask my good friend, Mrs. Hinkley, the one adventure that stands out in her mind more prominently than any other of the many she has had in her various trips to southern waters, she would immediately reply, "The fight between the shark and the tarpon at Knight's Key Trestle," and I almost agree with her. And this is the way it was:

One evening just about sunset "Hink" and I started for the trestle with the launch and two rowboats. Mrs. Hinkley came with us to watch from the launch what fun there might be. We anchored in a favorable position close to the trestle. The Captain went with "Hink" and I took Fred, one of the deck-hands. He was a strong, willing chap, interested and enthusiastic, but new to the game. We had hardly swung into place when there came that fascinating heavy strike followed by that ever-glorious jump. The ebb-tide was pretty heavy and I could see trouble ahead.

"Pull!" I shouted, and Fred lay back with a mighty effort—so mighty indeed that one of the oars sprang out of the oar-lock. He was so excited between the fish jumping and the possibility of being swept through the arches that he couldn't manage to get the oar back into place. Meanwhile I was having my own troubles, but there was only one thing to do. The oar must be replaced on the instant at all cost. So, keeping the rod up as best I could with my left hand, I turned around, grabbed the oar with my right and fortunately slipped it into place. This sounds easy, but with about one hundred and twenty-five pounds of lively tarpon on the other end of the line, aided by the excitement of the situation and a heavy tide, it was a fairly tough job.

"Pull!" I shouted. "Hi—ooh! Hi—ooh," I yelled as the fish came up again into the air.

Poor old Freddie! It was hard work and he was doing his best but making little or no head-way. The tarpon was almost through the arch.

"Pull!" I shouted again as I cast a hasty glance at his tense features and the perspiration pouring down his face. "Pull, pull!"

Slowly, inch by inch, we gained and good old Freddie stuck to his job. Finally we had the fish clear of the arches. We made our way by degrees close around the stern of the anchored launch up onto a shoal. As well as I could judge, the fish was about twenty yards from the launch in about three feet of water and about a hundred yards from where we were grounded. Suddenly Mrs. Hinkley stood up in the launch and waved her arms, frantically, and above the noise of the rushing tide, I could hear her words, "Shark, shark!" Then she pointed to the water and with her finger traced this cannibal right up to the spot where my fish was struggling.

Then ensued the most spectacular fight I ever witnessed. I was wholly unable to drag the fish away so I slackened my line and gave my fish full play. Up into the air he jumped, followed by a huge lunge from the shark, who in turn came half out of the water himself. Up and down they had it—over and under. I could see the shark strike and I could see the tarpon dart underneath. I could see the shark slash back and the tarpon jump into the air. Round and round in this shallow water, slashing and jumping, they fairly churned the water to a foam.

There was Mrs. Hinkley, jumping up and down, waving her arms, and calling at the top of her voice to the others for help. By this time Freddie had "come to" and joined the grand mêlée. His one idea seemed to be to frighten the fish. He stood up and all he could say was "Shoo! Shoo! Shoo!" and shake both arms at the shark. Unfortunately, however, it was a savage shark a hundred yards away instead of a flock of chickens.

I watched my chance and at the first opportunity I gave a mighty heave on the line and the tarpon, now almost exhausted, gave up and by some fortunate piece of luck I managed to pull him up into such shoal water that the shark couldn't follow.

"What will I do now?" whispered Fred, for his voice was gone.

"Get overboard with the gaff! Wade out to the fish and pull him in!" I replied.

He hesitated a minute.

"Oh, that's all right," I said; "the shark can't crawl up here."

So over he went and the fish was landed.

How it was the shark never got the tarpon is a mystery to me, because I never saw two dogs in a fight who seemed to be more mixed up than that tarpon and shark. "Oh, Wendell, Wendell, Wendell!" was all Mrs. Hinkley could say as we swung back to the launch. The fight had taken place almost under her very nose. She saw it all. Poor Freddie is teased to this day about his "shoo" at the shark, but he did a great job just the same, as it was one of my hardest fights against tide and fish.

From this stand one also fishes Sister Creek, which runs between Boot Key Harbor and the ocean, and while this "run" is invariably full of large fish it is seldom they take on account of the tremendous supply of mullets which are always in evidence.

The next "prospect" in line is Grouper Channel. I have already stated, and I shall emphasize the point again, that rowboats, and rowboats alone, must be used here in order to be assured of any measure of success. This is a small narrow channel running under the oval concrete arches at the westward end of the long Knight's Key Trestle. Being such a small, inconspicuous spot, it is seldom fished, but it has so happened that I have taken tarpon here when they would not strike at any other place. It is also one of the early places to fish with reasonable hope of success, oftentimes yielding some very large tarpon. The first fish that I

"FISHING SISTER CREEK"

Captain Butler Roberts, H. A. Forbes and C. D. Rafferty

—Page 84

[85]

raised last season was on March 3rd at this very place. That evening I started the season by landing three.

Grouper Channel stands out prominently in my mind as furnishing my record-size fish taken on rod and reel. This, however, was a fish of a different caliber. It was my first trip to Grouper Channel and we were fishing from a launch. Undoubtedly that accounted for the fact that we took no tarpon that night. It was so dark that it was almost impossible to see the trestle only a few feet away. My bait had swung down somewhere near one of the arches when suddenly it became fast. On the instant I sung out, "I'm caught to the pier," and the Captain circled back. Reaching the spot where the hook was fast, the Captain took hold of the line and tried to spring it loose.

"Why," he said, "there is no pier out here. We are ten feet away from the trestle. It must be a Jew-fish. That's what you've got." Sure enough the "pier" that I was fastened onto began to move slowly, then stopped. Any amount of pulling on my part didn't make the slightest impression. That fish moved only when he wanted to and stopped when he wanted to. In a half-hour's time I had perhaps moved him twenty feet away from the arches. In the next half-hour's time I had moved him a few feet more and into water that was about ten feet deep, and there he stuck. It was only after we rigged up the harpoon and jabbed it down in the direction of my line that we stirred him up sufficiently to lift him near to the surface. We finished the rest with the harpoon and brought to the boat a Jew-fish weighing, according to our estimate, between 450 and 500 pounds. Never again will I enjoy (?) a similar experience. He can have my hook and leader and will be welcome to it!

The next stopping-place is Bahia Honda— the biggest and the best—the place where "there are acres of 'em"—acres, however, that come and go. Here you can have the greatest fishing and the poorest; but, to my mind, it stands supreme. It is the place you eventually head for. You may try it and leave it, but you will always come back and try again for the big ones—the biggest of them all.

The most attractive place to anchor and the

most protected, although not the most convenient, is in the little run leading to the ocean just around the point to the eastward, named Little Bahia Honda Channel. This to me is one of the loveliest of all the harbors and incidentally is near the best of all the ocean beaches along the Keys and the best place for swimming.

Speaking of swimming, it seems to me this deserves a word or two of caution and suggestion. Having had considerable experience with sharks—having seen their savage attacks, having harpooned them right in the harbor close to the boat—I have no desire to plunge into the clear, attractive depths unless I can see the bottom plainly as well as see for a considerable distance on all sides. Some people laugh at the idea of caution. I trust they will always be in a position to laugh.

At all times, whether in deep or shallow water, one must guard most carefully against running into the "streamers" of those pretty blue and iridescent little "Portuguese Men-of-War" that are continually drifting by with the tide or wind. I have known of men who have

swum into one or dived onto one and suffered
so from the intense burning that they were
obliged to be taken to a hospital and treated
for relief. But these are easily seen and can
easily be avoided. The greatest danger of all
is wading in water that is cloudy. Never wade
unless you can see the bottom, otherwise you
might very readily step on a sting-ray. This is
a flat skate-like looking fish with a long rat-
tail. Its method of attack, or rather defense,
is with a group of sharp poisonous thongs or
spears at the base of the tail. To be poisoned
by a sting-ray is to be caused the most excru-
ciating agony.

And so carelessness in bathing spells danger.
Carefulness in bathing spells delight.

One begins his fishing on Bahia Honda at the
trestles. Please refer to the illustration. In the
middle of the picture is the so-called "center
arch." This is the highest construction and
the longest span. The best fishing is under the
five arches from the center to the eastward;
although sometimes the first three arches to
the west will yield fish. There is a little spot,
however, at the extreme western end which

"ONE BEGINS HIS FISHING ON BAHIA HONDA AT THE TRESTLES"

—Page 90

"AN EVENING'S CATCH AT BAHIA HONDA"
H. A. Forbes, General R. E. Wood and C. D. Rafferty

often yields a few small fish. Great care should be used, however, in fishing this place, as there are several sunken and dangerous piles. In approach one should keep close to the trestles.

Number Three is my favorite arch and here I have a sad and strange story to tell.

The fish were plentiful but the day had been too calm and the water too clear to produce any results. We had fished carefully all the morning and hadn't jumped a fish. Along about four o'clock in the afternoon, fully an hour or two before we usually start in, the Captain and I said good-by to the others, took a rowboat and slipped down to this Arch Number Three. The fish were there and occasionally were rolling. Quietly we held our place and were soon rewarded by a strike. There was a rush, a jump, and a handful of slack. "Missed, by Gosh!" So back again I went with better results. On the next fish, the line parted. We examined it very carefully. There had been no unusual strain, so we laid it, alas, to a weak spot in the line.

Again we "put out" and this time there was

a heavy strike, a slower but solid out-take, and up from the surface lunged a mighty fish.

"Heavens, Mr. Endicott," the Captain shouted, "that's the biggest fish I ever saw!" I know it was the biggest fish *I* ever saw. "For God's sake, don't lose him!"

Those were words indeed from the Captain. That massive tarpon was so large he couldn't even seem to clear himself. He made another break and again he couldn't clear. Then another rush. I brought into play everything I knew about the game. I wanted him and wanted him badly. I think I am too old a hand at the sport and the Captain too conservative to make too rash an estimate, but if ever a fish went well over two hundred and twenty-five pounds, that fish did. He was to be the prize of the country. He was to be the exhibition fish. But, and here goes the "but" again, the line suddenly broke and my prize—my exhibition tarpon—was gone, gone forever and ay. I felt more like crying than anything else. I certainly felt like a helpless little boy.

No words were spoken and I reeled in the few remaining yards of loose and wavy line.

It was the second time that my line had broken within the hour. "Let me look at the rod," said the Captain. "Damn that agate tip. It's broken." And sure enough the agate lining of the tip-ring was broken, leaving a sharp jagged edge. Somewhere, somehow, it had been broken. There was no excuse. We should have examined it beforehand, but it was too late and our "big chance" had slipped us by.

Forever Arch Number Three will have buried beneath its waters one of the biggest disappointments of my fishing career. There is one wonderful consolation, however, in the old saying, "There are just as good fish swimming in the sea to-day as ever have been caught." And this is without doubt true of Bahia Honda.

Even now, as I write of Bahia Honda, I can almost forget that disappointment and in its place have in my thoughts the memory of a strange beautiful night, weird and mysterious, never to be forgotten.

> Still as the shadows of those man-made arches
> Spanning the channels of deep Bahia Honda,
> Silent the tides flowing on towards the north'ard
> Into the dim mist of endless expanses.

Gray was the light from the stars in the heavens,
Shimmering only the path of a planet,
Mysterious hazes were curtained around us,
Night in its stillness was shrouded about us.

One dripping splash from a high jumping mullet,
Jumping for life from a swift darting monster,
Then all was quiet on deep Bahia Honda:
Awed were the souls of the two who sailed onward.

"HINK" AND HIS 77-POUND SAILFISH

—*Page* 101

CHAPTER IV

ACROBATS OF THE SEA

UNDOUBTEDLY the most sought-after game fish of the Florida East Coast is the famous sailfish. Rightfully can he be called "the acrobat of the ocean." There is no other fish I know of who carries with him so complete a "bag of tricks." At times, he is most finikin and tantalizing. Always is he capricious and at times voracious. His average weight is from thirty-five to sixty pounds. The largest fish that I have ever seen landed was one taken by my genial friend "Hink," tipping the scales at seventy-seven pounds.

The sailfish inhabits the Gulf Stream and is taken for the most part along its edge, just beyond that long sunken outer reef that runs parallel to the keys some five miles out at sea.

He is taken pretty generally along the whole coast as far north as Cape Canaveral, although my experiences have been confined to the grounds off Angel Fish Creek south along the keys to the grounds off Bahia Honda. It was on the edge of "the blue" off Tavernier that I had my first "adventure."

We had been fishing all the afternoon and had been kept busy with the barracuda and kingfish, which in itself is no mean sport but which is most annoying when one is "all set" for a sailfish.

In this connection I can remember fishing on another afternoon without a sign of any kind of fish when suddenly a few yards behind my bait appeared a sailfish. This put renewed courage into my wilted frame—when a large grouper rose, took the line and dived for the bottom. This was no time to spend ten or fifteen minutes in negotiating that heavy fish, so we boldly cut the line, rigged up anew and cast overboard. Although the whole transfer took less than a minute, Mr. Sailfish had departed and my afternoon's account was barren.

To continue with my story, the sun was getting low and we had decided to "pull in" and head for home. With the usual desire of the

"UP INTO THE AIR SHOT A LONG DARK FISH"

—Page 107

"APPARENTLY BALANCING HIMSELF ON THE END OF HIS
TAIL"

—Page 107

fisherman for "just one minute longer," I slowly and reluctantly began to reel in. The bait was within thirty feet of the boat when I heard a sudden exclamation from the Captain: "There he is—let him have it!" And before I knew what it was all about, there was a mad rush to the side.

Out went the line *whir! whir! whir!* and up into the air shot a long dark fish. My impression was folds of fluttering fins and a large beak. No sooner did he strike the water with a side-long splash than up he came again and this time performed to my amazement a most marvelous "stunt." Standing right up, almost at full length, apparently balancing himself on the end of his tail, he actually skipped with startling speed over the surface of the water, for a distance of fully sixty feet. Down he went and with amazing recovery he was up into the air again, twisting himself and throwing himself about in instantaneous maneuvers. One moment I was reeling in my line in frantic endeavor to take up all the slack from the onrushing fish; the next moment I was bracing myself against a long run of some hundred yards followed by a series of leaps in the air and another run.

"Look out, Captain! He's got about all my line!" I couldn't, I mustn't, miss that fish.

The Captain was ready on the moment to follow; but at this second the fish yielded to my pressure and stopped. Then followed some successful pumping which I felt meant the end of the contest. In, in, he came; but just as he got within fifteen feet of the boat, he decided that it didn't look good to him, and after making two surprisingly strong jumps, off he put out into the "blue." This run was shorter. He endeavored to jump again but this time he could only get his "head and shoulders" out. Slowly and carefully I worked him in toward the boat. Fearing some quick jump or rush, I eased off my tension drag to avoid any sudden and dangerous strain. It was fortunate indeed that I took this precaution, for just as we had him almost up to the boat, he lifted his head out of the water and made one last effort to throw the hook. The line eased off and the hook held. A few minutes more and I had him alongside.

"THIS TIME HE COULD ONLY GET HIS HEAD AND
SHOULDERS OUT"
—*Page* 108

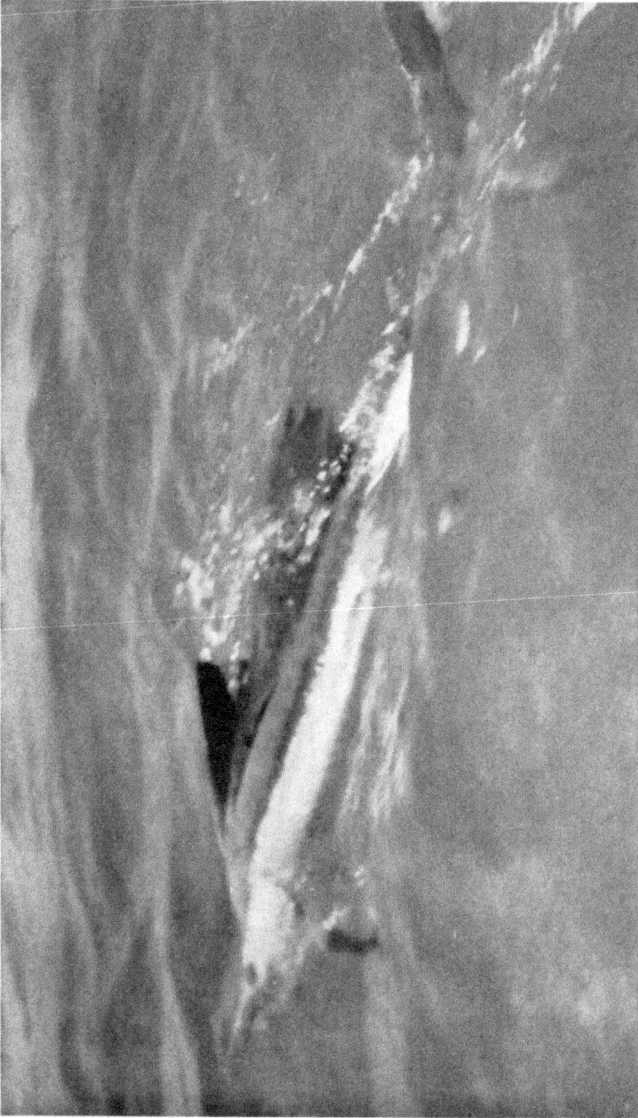

"SLOWLY AND CAREFULLY I WORKED HIM IN TOWARDS THE BOAT"
—*Page* 108

"HE LIFTED HIS HEAD OUT OF WATER AND MADE ONE
LAST EFFORT TO THROW THE HOOK"

—*Page* 108

Oh, the wonderful coloring of that fish! His large "sail" was an iridescent blue. Along his back were shadings of purple, green and gold, melting into the silver below; his sides were ribbed with yellowish silver.

"Oh, look!" I cried. "How glorious!"

With deliberation, the Captain reached over the side of the boat and grasped with gloved hand the long beak or sword of the fish, and pulled my prize into the boat.

Almost on the instant the colors of the fish faded. The beautiful shading changed to a dull slate on his back, and his sides and belly to a dull silver. He measured seven feet three inches, and weighed fifty-six pounds. In that forty minutes' fight he had come out of the water fifteen times.

As it proved afterward, I had indeed the "luck of a beginner" in having successfully hooked my first fish—or rather in having the fish successfully hook himself.

The question of hooking one's fish is, to my mind, one of the most interesting points, as well as the most important, in the game—the greater the skill the larger the bag.

The principle is this: The sailfish secures his food by first killing or disabling his prey with his sword and then taking it into his mouth. And so trolling along one will feel a tap, tap on one's line. This tapping is the sailfish attempting to "kill" the bait. Immediately you let out line, giving the impression to the fish that the bait is "killed" or "disabled." At that instant the fish may grab the bait and run. Let him have perhaps ten or twelve feet more; "feel" if he is on, then set the brakes and strike. If he is not there, hold the line for another tap— then let out quickly and "feel" for the fish. This "feel," instantaneous as it must be, is perhaps the hardest part of the "trick," for by that "feel" one must judge when to strike.

Oftentimes with a finikin or indifferent fish, one is obliged to let out a hundred feet or more before the "feel" tells you the fish has taken the bait firmly. On the other hand, some fish hit the bait hard—take it in all savageness and make a decisive run. There is no need of the "feel" here. You set your brakes and strike.

To me, it is the greatest kind of sport to watch the fish take the bait. You troll along

"THE CAPTAIN REACHED OVER THE SIDE OF THE BOAT
AND GRASPED WITH GLOVED HAND THE LONG
BEAK OR SWORD OF THE FISH"

—*Page* 115

[117]

with perhaps eighty or ninety feet of line on a free reel. Undoubtedly there will be two rods. The sailfish when swimming at a distance appears to be of mahogany color and this is what you watch for. Suddenly there is a cry from the Captain, "There he is—there he is!" and you catch a glimpse of a mahogany streak rising and falling with the waves just under the surface of the water. The fish may make a savage dart for your bait. He may take it or he may change his mind for no apparent reason and go for your companion's bait. I've seen fish sashay excitedly several times between the two baits before making up their minds which bait to take. At other times, a fish will steal up lazily back of the bait, look it over, follow it along, but make no effort to strike. I can remember one fish that followed my bait for two miles before he would take it. Of course, all that time we were exercising every trick we knew to tempt him to strike. We let out line and pulled it in, we criss-crossed, we jumped the bait, but it was not until we speeded up the boat to a decided pace that he did take the bait; but when he did make up his mind, he struck in all savageness. Sometimes a single fish will follow along that way and will not make any effort to strike until he "tolls up" another fish. Then apparently for fear his friend will secure the delectable morsel he makes his strike. Competition is a splendid thing even among sailfish, so in passing ahead of a school of fish, one is almost certain to get some action. Sometimes it means a double-header and that is indeed rare sport. Picture, if you can, two of these fish up in the air at the same time—rushing, rearing, tearing, jumping, splashing. Your fish crosses to the opposite side—the lines get twisted—you weave around with your companion—your fish goes off in one direction—while his goes in another. Perhaps you are forced to climb up around the bow. On goes the jumping—on goes the splashing—on goes the fighting—each fish playing a different game—each fish using different tactics.

One afternoon, and I shall never forget the sight, we passed in front of a school of fish. Two of us were fishing, and almost at the same instant we each had a strike. We hooked our

"SEVERAL TIMES I HAVE HOOKED FISH THAT HAVE STARTED OFF WITH ALL KINDS OF JUMPS AND TWISTS"

—*Page* 126

"THERE WAS A MAD RUSH TO THE SIDE"

fish and the fun began. I happened to look down and there, almost up to the boat, was a third sailfish. He was attracted by the "wooden whirler" which we were trolling a few feet astern. On the instant, I handed my rod to the Captain, grabbed an extra rod which was fortunately there ready and baited, cast overboard and in a second raised the fish. Now one sailfish creates a lot of interest and excitement, two sailfish create a riot of sport, but three sailfish all up in the air at one time fighting madly hither and thither, create a panic. Luck wasn't with us, however; we landed only two.

Perhaps my most spectacular fight with a sailfish was one morning while out with my friend "Hink." This particular fish in performing his various antics twice ran out the entire length of my three hundred yards of line. He was on the hook for fifty minutes and in that length of time came out of the water twenty-six times. But the unknown happened without any apparent reason. While on a slow steady pull he simply broke loose and departed. To see a fish disport himself in all known acrobatic feats, both in and out of the water, to be a contestant with a fish of such fighting and sporty proclivities, is indeed an adventure worth while.

Several times have I hooked fish that have started off with all kinds of jumps and twists and then suddenly stopped fighting and allowed themselves to be pumped to the boat. In such cases, they had so twisted themselves in the line and leader that they were held firm in a half circle, which made it impossible for them to struggle further.

One will find fishing in the Gulf Stream to be a most pleasurable experience. Sometimes the waters are as smooth as any forest pond, and then again the current of the stream, flowing perhaps four miles an hour against a northeast blow, will kick up such a sea that everything must be well tied down. Occasionally have I been "out there" when a companion fishing boat not one hundred yards away would disappear quite out of sight—hidden in some valley of waves.

"Snappy sport, I calls it," says "Hink" fast to a sailfish as he is tossed first mountain high, then valley deep. Confidentially, "Hink" has

"SNAPPY SPORT, I CALLS IT', SAYS 'HINK' AS HE IS TOSSED MOUNTAIN HIGH"

—*Page* 126

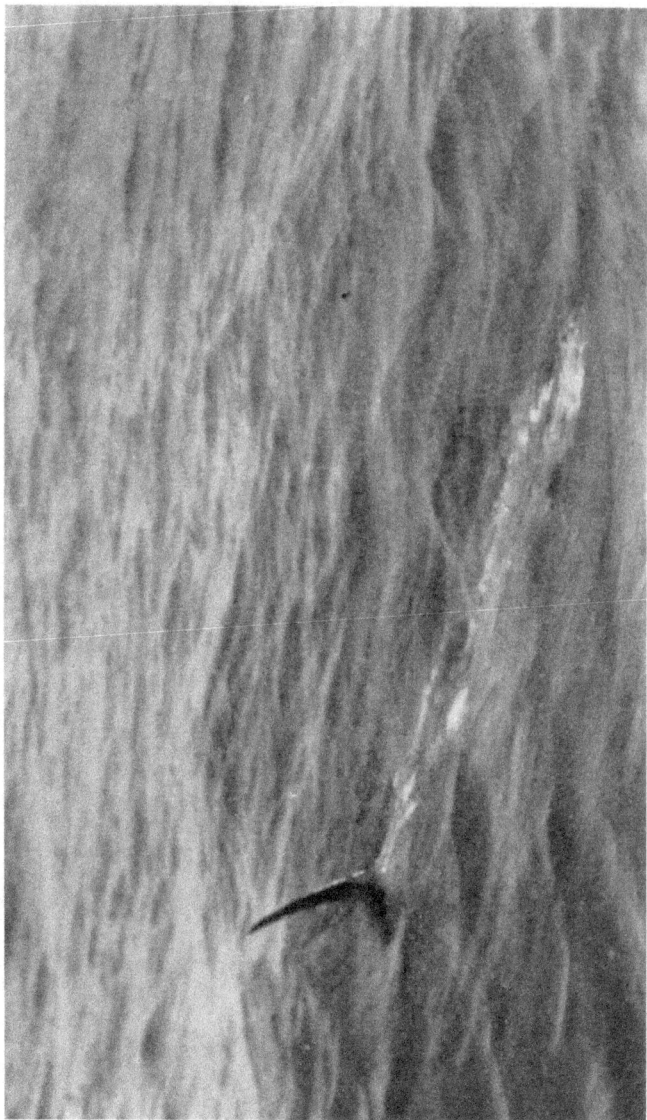

"OF COURSE YOUR FIRST THOUGHT IS TO WATCH FOR THE NARROW SPIKE OF HIS TAIL CUTTING THE SURFACE OF THE WATER"

—Page 131

a little more "ballast" to keep him anchored than most of us.

But mild as a rule, one cruises along ever on the alert to see and enjoy the great variety of sea life and witness the endless fish tragedies that are ever being enacted before one's very eyes—the survival of the fittest.

Of course your first thought is to watch for a sailfish jumping or the narrow spike of his tail cutting the surface of the water, whereupon you rush with all speed to this spot in the hope of attracting him to your lure. How fascinating it is to see those long, straight, lanky fish throw themselves slantwise up into the air and, seemingly without bending, fall back with a heavy splash! Apparently they do this for sport, for I have seen a fish make as many as eighteen jumps in quick succession.

Here you will see a cero mackerel shoot up into the air; there you will see a kingfish jump clear and clean of the water; in toward the reefs you will see a big school of balaos break the surface in a cloud of spray followed by some heavy strike of barracuda or grouper. If you look sharply, you may see a big loggerhead turtle floating lazily on the surface—but quickly submerging if you get too close.

At times, you will see a monster devil-fish, weighing perhaps 2,000 pounds or more, throw himself into the air and fall back with a tremendous splash. You will see a school of porpoise rolling and blowing in the distance. Occasionally, you will see a porpoise jump like a fish fully eight or ten feet straight into the air. Just once in the Gulf Stream have I seen a sun-fish—but that was enough to secure a good specimen with the harpoon. Strange indeed is this curiously shaped fish, weighing perhaps 400 pounds—big as to body but inconceivably small as to mouth. Often you will see monster sharks cruising along with those sharp knife-like fins protruding above the surface.

We had one day a most wonderful demonstration of the keenness of scent of a shark. The water was calm and we could see for a long distance anything that disturbed the surface of the water. We had been trolling along slowly for some time with no action, when we caught up with and passed at about thirty feet abreast of us a huge hammerhead shark. We

"HOW FASCINATING IT IS TO SEE THOSE STRAIGHT, LANKY FISH THROW THEMSELVES SLANTWISE UP INTO THE AIR"

—Page 131

[133]

"JUST ONCE IN THE GULF STREAM HAVE I SEEN A SUN-
FISH—BUT THAT WAS ENOUGH TO SECURE A
GOOD SPECIMEN"

—Page 132

[135]

had out perhaps eighty feet of line. The bait must have passed no closer than thirty feet from the shark. Remember that this bait had been in the water for nearly an hour and must have been pretty well washed out, but hardly had this bait passed by the shark when he bristled up and came apparently to alert attention. He waited a few seconds and then shot off to the side, crossing the trail of this small piece of bait. Like a hunting dog, he turned and criss-crossed the trail several times until finally he located it definitely and then, as straight as a die and putting on speed, he swam right up to the bait. The bait happened to be a small clean strip of mackerel belly without blood and with its hour's washing must have left in the water a minimum amount of scent, proving the shark's keenness of smell.

Another demonstration of the savageness of these prowling ever-ready cannibals of the sea came one morning when we were just landing a sailfish. The fish had been brought along-side and the Captain had reached over the side and had lifted the fish, holding it against a few last struggles. Suddenly from out of the deep rose a gray ghost-like monster and with one rush attacked the sailfish. In an instant the Captain was left with half a sailfish in his hand. It was a horrible and sad thing to have witnessed, for in a second more we would have unhooked the sailfish and have sent him back to his happy home. "I'll fix that shark," said the Captain, and in a minute he was ready with the harpoon. The cannibal, anxious for another mouthful, came back, in fact, came boldly right up to the boat, and on that instant the Captain plunged the "iron" into him firmly and surely and fourteen feet of shark headed for the bottom of the Gulf Stream. I doubt if a yoke of oxen could have stopped the rush of that powerful animal. There had been no time to attach a buoy to the end of the line and all efforts to change the course of the shark failed—the line fairly "sang" over the cleat and when the end of the line was reached, it snapped like the merest thread. Inasmuch as the unexpected always happens, one should always be ready with harpoon fully rigged and securely attached to a buoy. If I had always followed this sage advice, the sea would have been rid of several

"THE CAPTAIN HAD LIFTED THE FISH AGAINST A FEW
LAST STRUGGLES"

—Page 137

of those mean, vicious, repulsive beasts, which are, as far as I know, to-day free to continue their prowling and preying on injured and helpless inhabitants of the deep. An autopsy at one time performed on one of these sharks disclosed a half-digested piece of fish, several bones of some animal, several handfuls of old feathers, two whole crawfish, and a whole horseshoe crab measuring fully eight inches across the back. Why that sharp dagger-like tail of the horseshoe crab didn't puncture the shark's "in'ards" is more than I can say.

Speaking of releasing fish, this is something all true sportsmen appreciate in these southern waters. Occasionally, however, there is some fish hog who feels it necessary to bring "home" every fish that is landed. What can he do with them? Nothing—nothing but throw them overboard—food for crabs and sharks. Oh, the pity of that needless waste! What if the fish are plentiful? What if the supply seems limitless? Haven't we had in this country many sad examples where waste and needless slaughter have ruined this or that hunting or fishing ground, where all lack of sportsmanlike intelligence has depleted this or that species?

I have a vision before me now of an amazingly large string of fish brought in from the Gulf Stream and hung on some old pier. There were in that string three sailfish, eight or ten barracuda, probably six or more grouper and a couple of amber-jacks. There they were left in the sun to rot, and all for no purpose.

It is true a barracuda, with his vicious sharp dog-like teeth, is hard to release, but even this can be done with a bit of patience and care. It is seldom, however, that a sailfish cannot readily be unhooked and sent on his way rejoicing.

Our party has taken as high as fifty-eight sailfish in one season of about a month's intermittent fishing and I think it of interest to state that we had the pleasure of releasing about fifty of that catch.

"He who fights and runs away,
Will live to fight another day,
And further yet to make amends
The chances are he'll bring his friends."

I have been asked many times, "Which would you rather take, a sailfish or a tarpon?" And I always hesitate in answering this question. When a sailfish is "tapping" my bait, when I am trying to set the hook at just the right time into that small bony mouth, when I am treated to a "tail dance" or a series of acrobatic stunts, I say to myself, "What could be greater sport?" When a tarpon makes a heavy strike and a mad rush followed by that spectacular leap into the air, when that glorious "Silver King" shakes his head like an angry bulldog, when he falls back into the water again with a mighty splash and my line goes whirring out in the wake of a powerful dash, I say to myself again, "What could be more thrilling, more wonderful!"

And so I doubt if I am able to answer that question in all honesty. In this instance I certainly have a vacillating opinion. Why not let that remain a question for you to answer for yourself?

CHAPTER V

ADVENTURES ON THE REEF

BY no means is the sport of fishing in Florida confined to the tarpon and the sailfish.

Here are the channels, the shoals, the reefs, the Gulf Stream, teeming with countless varieties of fish both great and small—fish of the rarest coloring and beauty; fish unique in shape and size; fish most interesting in habit and play; fish most delectable to the inner man.

I know of several little spots about two hundred yards from the westward end of Trestle No. 2, on either the gulf or ocean side, where one is sure to find an interesting collection of small bottom fish. Let him not despise this tamer line of sport, but rather let him enjoy it in its beautiful and surprising variety, while supplying the ingredients for many a delicious breakfast or luncheon. In a half-hour's time, he will have his "well" completely stocked with

"THE PELICAN—THAT INTERESTING, WISE OLD BIRD"

—*Page* 147

[145]

"MY FRIEND, JOHN HALEY, WHO HAS BROUGHT IN A
'FEW EXTRA FOR BILL'"

[146]

many delectable pan fish, and while he is about it let him lay by a few extra for Bill the Pelican —that interesting wise old bird who is always sure to welcome him along the Keys.

First of all come the blue, the yellow, and the gray grunt. His manifestions proclaim his name. Indeed he announces himself quite audibly with his *grunt, grunt, grunt.*

Then come the several species of porgies. Then the really beautiful yellow and black pork-fish; the sheepshead; the hog-fish; the margate-fish; the sailor's choice, the fascinating gray and white spotted angel-fish; the blue runner; and numerous other beautifully marked and interesting species. If you don't watch out, perhaps you will be unfortunate enough to pull in a wriggling and repulsive snake-like moray. Be careful he doesn't bite, inflicting a poisonous sting.

Some day along in the channels you will troll with light tackle for the Spanish mackerel— a sporty little chap on a rod, a delicious little chap on the table. Then again you may glide along by the trestles and if the strong, fighting, gamy but insistent Jack Cavallas do not take

all your bait and time, you will land an eight-
or ten-pound mangrove snapper or a beautiful
pink mutton-fish. While the Jack is given his
liberty, the snapper and especially the mutton-
fish is brought home for "baking purposes." I
think it is worthy of note that my friend,
Harold Keith, landed one evening what I believe to be a record mangrove snapper which
tipped the scales at 35 pounds.

A grouper of almost any size is apt to be in
line for a delicious chowder. A sharp-toothed
barracuda—"the Tiger of the Sea"—is often
waiting "around the corner"; and a mackerel
shark—curses on him!—is always ready to give
you all the fight you want. Already have I
hinted at the muscle-tiring Jew-fish. Avoid
him if you can.

A day out on the reef is an adventure to be
long cherished. As a matter of advice to a
beginner, nothing could get his "hand" in
better, nothing could teach him more as to the
ways of rod, reel and action, than just such a
day's sport. Even to the veteran a "reef day"
never fails to produce some new experience,
some added pleasure.

"THEN AGAIN YOU MAY GLIDE ALONG BY SOME TRESTLE"

—*Page* 147

"A SHARP-TOOTHED BARRACUDA, THE TIGER OF THE SEA"

—Page 148

[151]

Perhaps when you "put out" for the reef, the water will be calm and clear and on the way you will pass over some "rock beds." These are the nautical gardens. And gardens they are indeed. No hand of man ever wrought such indescribable displays of artistry. Looking through glass-bottomed pails, you gaze at untold beauty. There you will see delicately conceived sprays and trees of coral growth. You will see yellow and purple lacelike fans gently swaying with the moving tide. You will see fantastically shaped and beautifully colored sea-plant growth, and slowly passing in and out will be myriads of small highly colored fish—perhaps the most beautiful being the parrot-fish with his peacock shadings. You will see, too, the long feelers of the crawfish protruding from some hidden crevice. And if you look sharply, you can make out a part of some huge Jew-fish who has squeezed himself flatwise under a protecting coral shelf. All this to me is outstanding in its marvelous and indescribable beauty. Who wouldn't take a trip of many miles just to feast his eyes on such a picture of God's great handiwork?

Out there on the reef the fun begins with a bang. You can see the bottom. You can see the fish make for your bait. You may have raised a savage barracuda or a hungry grouper. Perhaps a cero mackerel has seized your bait, and if he doesn't look out he in turn will serve as bait for some ever-watchful barracuda. This has happened many times. Picture, if you can, having quite a struggle with a lively mackerel —when suddenly there is a mighty splash and a heavy rush and instead of negotiating a six-pound fish, the scene is instantly changed to a thirty or forty pound "tiger."

The strongest fighter of all the reef fish is the amber-jack; in fact, he is the strongest fighter for his size there is. His average weight is from twenty to fifty pounds but occasionally one is taken as high as eighty pounds. At all events you can prepare for a good, long, heavy contest. When you do have an amber-jack on your line, it is but a simple matter to toll up from the deep a few of his friends, who are always obliging enough to take any other live bait that may be offered them. In fact, they

"LOOKING THROUGH GLASS-BOTTOMED PAILS YOU GAZE
AT UNTOLD BEAUTY"

—Page 153

"YOU MAY HAVE RAISED A SAVAGE BARRACUDA"

—*Page* 154

[157]

will take a live bait almost from your very hands.

Perhaps you may slip out a little farther into the Gulf Stream to land a kingfish—that worthy fighter who can well be classed among the "sports." At times I have seen him strike at the bait with such force and speed that he would shoot into the air as high as fifteen feet. When properly cooked I hold the kingfish as among the best for household purposes.

On the edge of "the blue"—in fact, in line with sailfishing—you may enjoy a bonito—a strong gamy little fish of eight to fifteen pounds, clean and firm in its coloring of blue; or you may negotiate a tuna, belonging to that famous game fish family. Seldom, however, is he taken in these waters heavier than ten or fifteen pounds.

Then, if you are lucky, you will be treated to one of the real thrills of Gulf Stream fishing. Seldom is he caught but never does he fail to test the skill and muscle of the fisherman. This is the wahoo, the swiftest of all large fish. My first experience came one afternoon when we were out in the Stream seeking a wily sailfish. Things had been pretty quiet for some time and I was perhaps a bit listless and inattentive. Suddenly there was a bang—a strike of such force it brought me to my feet. With the speed of lightning my line shot out, *whir, whir, whir!* The fish, a stranger to me, just plowed the surface of the water in a mad rush headed for somewhere.

"Wahoo!" shouted the Captain. "Watch out! He'll take your line!"

What could I do? I might just as well have tried to stop a train of cars; but the Captain, an old hand at the game, knew the trick and was ready with the needed help. There wasn't time to turn the boat, so he put on full steam astern. This helped some, and by the fortune of luck the wahoo changed his mind just in time and yielded somewhat to my pressure. Between the backing of the boat and a limited amount of pumping, I gained back some of my line, but only to be rewarded with another "plowing race" driven by a bolt of lightning. It was a hard, fast and furious fight, but everything held, my endurance included, and in due

"ONE OF THE MANY VESSELS THAT ARE CONSTANTLY
PLOWING ALONG TOWARD THE SOUTH"
—*Page* 163

time I brought to gaff a "new variety," a wahoo of 60 pounds. Now, with the wahoo, guard him carefully and bring him home. Boiled wahoo with egg sauce for dinner is indeed a dish "fit for a king," but its delicacy prepared in this way is strongly contested by the fish cakes that a wise and competent chef will offer up for breakfast the following morning.

Slip out into "the blue" still farther and perhaps you will be rewarded with a dolphin—the most highly and beautifully colored of all the fish. He, too, is a "jumper" of no mean speed and strength. One gasps indeed when that beauty of light greens and gold flashes up into the air and sunlight.

And so you can spend your days on the reef and Gulf Stream ever seeking and ever finding adventure in life and beauty, and as you turn toward the sunset and head for home you will wave your hand to a great day's sport—and a good-by or "bon voyage" to one of the many vessels that are constantly plowing along toward the south—bound for unknown ports—perhaps to the tropics, perhaps to the distant Orient.

CHAPTER VI

THE CAPRICIOUS BONEFISH

REFER to any unabridged dictionary, look up the words *capricious, timid, suspicious* and *finikin,* make a list of these four with all their synonyms, and then apply that list against the bonefish and perhaps then you will begin to have a description of his character.

Consider the monk in his hours and hours of prayerful solitude and, like him, while not obliged perhaps to resort to sackcloth and ashes, nevertheless you must be prepared for hours and hours, yea, even days and days, of solitude in waiting, if perchance it is your desire to capture "His Shyness" the bonefish. As for the prayer part of it, begin by a supplication for a rising tide at just the time you want to fish, as it is imperative to be at the bank or chosen spot shortly after the first of the flood. It is then that the bonefish is supposed

"HIS SHYNESS THE BONEFISH"

—*Page* 164

to make his way from the channels up onto the banks in search of certain delicate tidbits. Then pray for a windless day, or at least that "your spot" be protected from a heavy wind. Rough sea or disturbed water is very repelling to bonefish sensibilities. Of course there mustn't be any fleeting clouds to cast annoying shadows upon the waters, and as for pelicans flying about, that must be absolutely prohibited. Forthwith, then, with everything favorable— spot, tide, wind, sun, and birds—pray above all that a bonefish will appear and pray still harder that he will come your way.

Of course, there are times when he will do the unexpected—"kick over the traces," so to speak, and forget himself and his usual ways. Sometimes you will find him reasonably commonplace, but such times are rare indeed.

And yet how quickly are all the hours of watchful waiting forgotten when the golden moment comes, for in that golden moment the patient fisherman is rewarded beyond his fondest dreams. The taking of a bonefish is a rare, choice, exhilarating experience. It is "the champagne of fishing."

With everything right, you set out for the bonefish bank. Perhaps you pole around a bit, hoping to see a distant tail flick in the sunlight, or a bluish shadow in the water, giving you then a possible clue as to where the fish are feeding. More than likely, you see nothing, so you stake out your boat in that possible twelve to twenty inches of water, cast your line toward a favorable-looking sand spot sixty or seventy feet away, sit down and wait. You needn't hurry to "take in" the surroundings—there'll be plenty of time for that. After a while your thoughts wander to a smoke; you take out your pipe—look out, don't hit it against the boat, for perhaps a fish may, in his mysterious way, be in the neighborhood. A half-hour has passed and you decide to reel in and see how your bait looks. Fortunately you did, for the hook is bare. You have supplied a dinner to some crafty crab.

Quietly you reach down in the boat and pick up a piece of lead which you place carefully on your knee; then you select a favorable looking hermit crab, reach for a hammer and with muffled blows break the shell, toss the pieces

"YOU STAKE OUT YOUR BOAT, SIT DOWN AND WAIT"

—*Page* 168

gently overboard for chum, bait up and cast again.

So silently and unseen can these fish work over the shoals that before you know it you may feel the slightest kind of a tug on your line. You strike, hardly believing that there could be anything on the other end larger than a minnow. Then, like a shot out of a gun, this fish makes a "straight away." The reel fairly sings and your whole being is thrilled with the speed and brilliance of that dash. On—on— he goes for a hundred yards, yes, perhaps two hundred yards. Then, "mirabile dictu," something amazing happens. Suddenly and without warning, he turns and with equal speed dashes right back toward the boat. Reel, reel, reel as best you can. Another sudden shift and he's off in a different direction—another turn and another run. Perhaps by this time he yields a bit to the rod and you work him toward the boat. "But what," says he, "is a boat?" and lightning is again brought into play.

Surely, without question of a doubt, this sporty thoroughbred stands at the head in speed

—no other fish can "touch" him. He is supreme. Again you work him in slowly and with great care. This time he changes his direct line of flight to that of describing circles around the boat. Lesser and lesser are those circles and at last you have him at hand, exhausted by his brilliant, sporty fight. Mailed glistening silver describes his firm solid body. The most delicious of all the fish describes his palatable qualities.

The fisherman has then been inoculated with the bonefish germ.

No tarpon or sailfish will ever drive away the desire to "take just one more—somehow at some time."

Six bonefish are the most we have ever taken on any one tide, and nine pounds is my personal record, although I have known of several larger fish having been taken by some of the bonefish enthusiasts of Long Key.

I can cite quite a different experience from the above, which happened to me on the Knight's Key bank one warm calm morning. It took us some time to locate a fish, and after we had poled around for nearly an hour we

"SIX BONEFISH ARE THE MOST WE HAVE EVER TAKEN ON ANY ONE TIDE"

—*Page 172*

saw in the distance a "bluish shade" (for that
is their almost transparent appearance in the
water). We made a cast and unfortunately, as
it seemed to us, the bait fell too close to the
fish. We looked for a swirl and a hasty depar-
ture; but apparently on this particular morning Mr. Bonefish wasn't in a fretful frame of
mind. Slowly and unconcernedly he worked his
way up to the bait, looked it over a bit and went
on. Just at the right we saw three fish working
our way. Over the bait they passed with no
more interest than if my lure had been a mere
stone. Quickly I reeled in and made a successful cast about fifteen feet ahead of them. Up
they came, but still they wouldn't take. We
pulled up and poled after the slowly moving
fish, stopping now and then to cast the bait in
their path. Naturally we created some disturbance, but against all their principles, they
seemed oblivious to our presence and noise. We
made at least six casts before one finally decided
to take advantage of my offering. That morning we saw and chased twelve fish and at no
time did they display the usual sensitive wariness.

It is interesting to compare the difference when you stop to think that sometimes simply the shadow of a gull passing over a bank will send a bonefish helter-skelter for deep water.

Sometimes you can locate these fish feeding near a sandy beach and by sneaking up and crawling around you can place your bait in such a favorable position as to get almost immediate action.

But "waiting" as a rule is the watchword for the bonefish aspirant, and I have known an aspirant to be so inoculated by the germ that he has cast to the four winds of heaven with a mere snap of his fingers some almost sure opportunity to capture a sailfish or tarpon and instead has sat uneventfully on a bank for three successive days—flood-tide or ebb-tide, clouds, birds or wind, all having no effect on him. He had nothing but patience and a hope that on the morrow a fish would come his way.

The bank off Rodriguez Key is one of the best spots for bonefish. The banks around Trestle No. 2 are popularly fished from Long Key. There are several particularly good places around Tom's Harbor. Another hope-

"ONE OF THE MOST FAVORABLE BANKS IS THAT ONE RIGHT OFF BOOT KEY"

Captain Starck and Joseph B. Russell, Jr.

—*Page* 179

ful spot is on the shoal at Key Vaca Channel, and perhaps one of the most favorable banks is that one right off Boot Key. There are many spots along the beaches both known and undiscovered that offer possibilities.

I can remember very well one afternoon taking my little daughter out for a stroll along a beach. We batted down some cocoanuts, we picked some shells, we built sand castles and tossed pebbles at the big barracuda that lazily drifted close to shore. Instinctively my eye caught the motion of three "bluish streaks." Could it be possible? Could those streaks be bonefish? I watched them dig their noses into the sand and flick their tails above the surface —stand on their heads as it were. I threw a bit of stick high over the water to imitate a bird. Like a flash they were gone. "Stupid," said I. "Why didn't I run back to the boat for my tackle?" Hardly had I condemned myself with those words when I saw five more fish slowly working up the shore. This time I left instructions with my little daughter and ran for home. It was a long pull and consumed a lot of valuable time, but the Captain, as always, was ready with rod and bait and in three-quarters of an hour, we had returned and found our friends still feeding close at hand. I was rewarded for my efforts.

Ah! that glorious run—that brilliant fight. I quaffed indeed the "champagne cup" of fisherman's joy.

"WE BUILT SAND CASTLES"

"WE GATHERED SHELLS"

—*Page* 179

CHAPTER VII

ADVENTURES WITH THE HARPOON

FOR the most part the harpoon is incidental to the rod, to be used at unexpected moments, to be the means of capturing some new variety of monster that may at any moment appear from the mysterious deep or that may perchance be in your line of progress, to be used to save from an attacking cannibal shark some brave fighting sailfish or tarpon. In fact, the harpoon is a necessary and useful adjunct to any fishing outfit along the Florida Keys. Used, however, as the "chief implement of war" and under the right conditions the harpoon can supply any sportsman with real melodramatic adventure of thrill and excitement as well as a certain amount of danger resulting from a careless movement or slip.

To enter upon such an adventure one wants a reasonably smooth, calm sea, clear water, clear sky and a favorable stretch of shoals.

One also wants a sure footing, a good balance, and a quick eye. Together with all these, one wants a good launch and a keen captain ready for fight and action.

I can truthfully say that harpooning is no child's play but rather an adventure worthy of any man's skill.

Picture, if you can, an adventurer standing up on the bow of a launch—cruising here and there over the shoals—hunting and looking for some monster fish—ready for the chase—keen with excitement to reach a favorable position—filled with impatience to make the telling throw. You realize that it is all up to you whether you succeed or not. You realize that by your aim and skill the "iron" goes true or misses the mark and buries itself in the sand or coral bottom.

To those who may not be fully acquainted with the principle of the harpoon, it might be helpful to note this short description:

There is a double or tandem arrow-like dart called a toggle, perhaps some five inches long. In between the two arrow-heads is a small parallel socket and ring. A twelve-foot pole with a soft iron rod some twelve inches long is

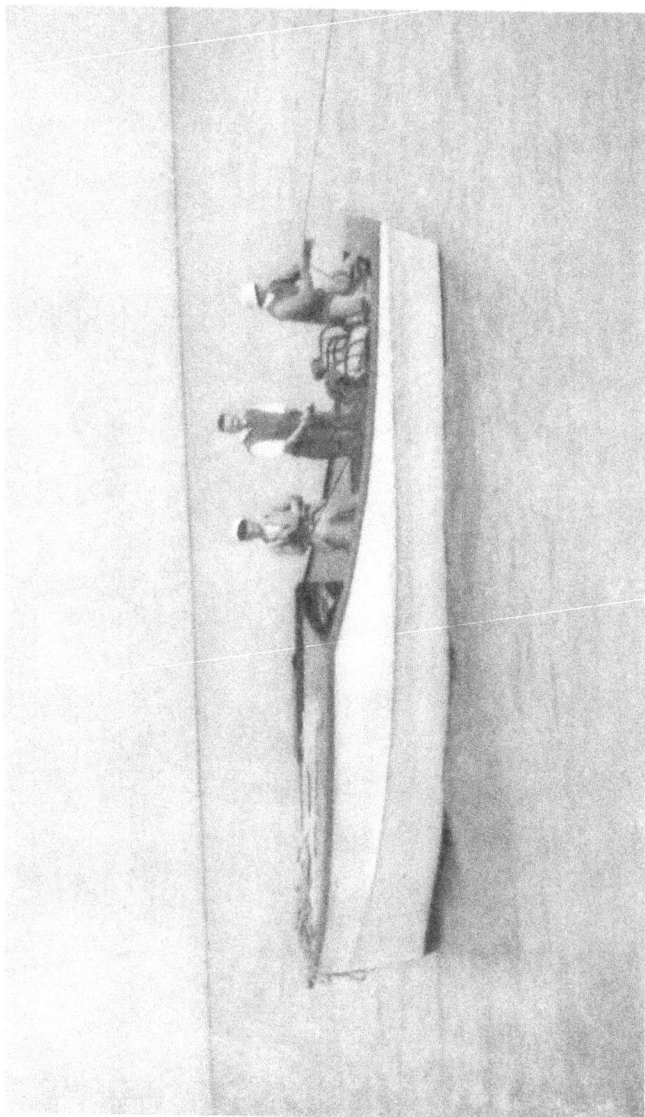

—Page 184

"THIS IS NO CHILD'S PLAY"

Captain Butler Roberts, Russell Nourse and Joseph Russell, Jr., fast to a whip-ray

"PICTURE, IF YOU CAN, STANDING ON THE BOW OF A
LAUNCH, CRUISING HERE AND THERE OVER
THE SHOALS"

—*Page* 184

fitted loosely into the socket. A rope about the size of a clothes-line is attached to a short wire cable which in turn is fastened to the ring between the arrow-heads. The line is brought taut with a couple of half-hitches around the farther end of the pole, the effect being that the sharp arrow-head or toggle is a part of the long pole. This pole carries the aim of the throw and gives weight to the force of the stroke. On striking the fish the soft iron rod bends, releases the pole from the socket and leaves the rope attached to the toggle firmly imbedded in the fish. The half-hitches are automatically unfastened, the pole floats away, and the contestant is left to negotiate the line and fighting fish as best he can.

Although I had planned to confine the adventures of harpooning to one chapter I find that unconsciously I have already woven stories of harpooning and sharks into my tales of the tarpon and the sailfish and even into my advice on swimming. But this must necessarily be so, because wherever there is a tarpon you will find a shark; wherever there is a sailfish, you will find a shark; wherever there is a shark you think of a harpoon. It is my opinion that the man of mildest disposition would willingly, yes, happily, wage war on those vicious, cruel and repulsive cannibals.

In days of old I have heard varying tales of the danger or the harmlessness of sharks. Some sage fisherman would tell a direful tale; some wise raconteur would laugh at the idea. "Oh, no," said he; "you'll find a shark more frightened of you than you are of him. He'll never attack." And I was left a doubting Thomas—doubting, that is, until one fine day I decided the question for myself.

I was standing in the bow looking for sharks. I was ready with the harpoon and eager for a shot, when suddenly I caught sight of a shadowy ghost-like body moving along slowly in about six feet of water. I gave the signal to the Captain, glanced carefully to see that the rope was free, then gave my attention to the chase. That ghost proved to be a twelve-foot tiger or blue-nose shark—one of the most vicious of them all. As we came closer, he moved on a little faster. Soon we were going parallel to him at quite a pace—keeping him inshore.

"ONE OF THESE VICIOUS, CRUEL AND REPULSIVE
CANNIBALS"

—*Page* 190

"A 'CLOSE-UP' OF A CANNIBAL"

"The raconteur was right," thought I; "the shark prefers to run."

Soon, however, the shark apparently changed his mind; the race did not appear to interest him and he slowed down. On the instant, the Captain changed our course and swung the boat toward our prey. It was not an easy shot, but I felt I was near enough and cast the harpoon, hitting him lightly but just enough to hold. On that very instant, before I could even collect my senses, this shark turned and made one ferocious charge on the boat. He hit the side with considerable force, turned and departed. The iron pulled out and the shark was free. Later that evening when I examined our boat, I saw several fresh gashes on the side and from one gash I extracted a broken tooth. The raconteur was wrong. Here was a shark, mad with fury, who attacked to kill.

What if I had lost my balance and fallen overboard? What if the outrushing line had snarled around my foot and dragged me into the water? Would that ferocious cannibal have turned and fled? Would I have been left free and easy in the water? Did I need any more proof to make up my mind as to the temper of the shark?

"Perhaps it was because he was wounded," one might say, "and a wounded beast is always more ferocious." In answer, let me relate this tale:

The circumstances were quite similar to the adventure above, but this time the Captain was on the bow with harpoon in hand and I was in another boat some few hundred yards away. I saw the Captain throw the "iron." He missed. Having no further interest, I turned to 'tend to matters of my own. In a few seconds I was conscious of considerable excitement in the Captain's boat. My little daughter, who was with the Captain, was jumping about and running from one side to the other. I hastened over to their boat and this is what the Captain said: "We had been chasing a huge leopard shark for quite some time—at last I took a chance shot and missed. I never even scratched him, but suddenly he turned, made one rush and a mighty leap right for us. He threw his whole body fully three feet out of the water—his jaws were wide open and never have

"THERE I SAW A JAGGED HOLE FULLY TEN INCHES LONG
AND FOUR INCHES BROAD"

—*Page* 199

I seen such a mad, wicked picture of fury. He hit us like a ton of bricks. Now look at this," and he pointed over the side. There I saw a jagged hole fully ten inches long and four inches broad right through the side of the boat. The boat was built of ⅞-inch cedar, well braced and of recent construction and Mr. Shark had in his ferocious attack smashed it as you might smash a shell. Fortunately, it was just above the water line, otherwise there might readily have been another story to tell. I took a picture of the hole. I only wish it might have been a movie.

Now, Mr. Raconteur, was this a case of a shark so frightened that he wanted to swim away—that he had no courage to attack? Come to the South, say I, associate a bit with these monsters and I am quite convinced that you will have with me a wholesome respect for the ways and habits of a shark.

I can remember one afternoon on Bahia Honda when the harpoon did good service to a friend in need. The Captain and I were fishing by the trestle and my companion was in another launch farther out in the bay. He was quite some distance away. We heard him give the "tarpon yell" and we saw the fish leap into the air. It was a pretty sight to watch at that distance. Soon we saw them put on speed and head for the shoal. What did this mean? Why were they risking all that extra and dangerous strain on rod and line? Then we saw the reason. Steadily moving and slowly gaining on the leaping fish was a tell-tale fin—the fin that sends a shudder down one's spine. They were trying to drag the fish out of the clutches of the shark. In a second I reeled in my line. In another second I was at the wheel and the Captain was poised on the bow, harpoon in hand. "Open her up!" he shouted, and we shot ahead. Could we make it in time? We could see the shark sheering, now on one side, now on the other. The fish had dragged out nearly 300 yards of line. It would be a straight pull in a few seconds. Would the line break first? Would we get there first? These were our thoughts as we surged ahead. It looked to us as if the shark was fairly on top of the tarpon and we would be too late.

By this time the fish, half drowned, was

"AND WE IN TURN RIGHT BEHIND THE SHARK"

—Page 203

being dragged on its side at considerable speed. The shark was right behind the tarpon and we in turn right behind the shark, who incidentally paid not the slightest attention to us. Out shot the harpoon, true and firm,—down went the shark. He was a monster hammerhead, fully fourteen feet long. It was a close call, but we won.

It was on one afternoon outside of Trestle No. 2, that we harpooned the biggest monster of them all. We were headed for the reef, when up into the air shot some huge thing, black and flat looking.

"What's that?" I cried. "It looks like a jumping island."

"Devil-fish," was the reply.

Ever on the alert, ever ready for adventure, cat-like in his jump, the Captain sprang to the bow, harpoon in hand, and in a second he was giving me directions—this way or that—faster or slower. Thus did we maneuver for striking position.

At last we had it right and the Captain let go. It was a sure shot and we were fast to a moving, tearing, splashing, fighting, whirling monster of a fish. I jumped to the bow, ready with the second harpoon. Off he plunged. We didn't dare put on too much pressure. We didn't want the toggle to pull out. In some marvelous way, however, the Captain at last worked us up near enough for me to shoot. Then we felt better. We had the fish on two lines. For nearly a mile, he pulled our 27-foot launch through the water with the greatest ease.

"I hope he stays on the surface," said the Captain. "If he sounds we'll never get him."

On, on, he went, swimming with that curious butterfly-like stroke of his huge side flippers.

"Hink" was at hand to join in the excitement, and with his usual good judgment he eased alongside and handed me his .303 rifle. The sea was rough, which added to the problem, but in due time and with Herculean efforts on the part of the Captain, we worked ourselves near enough to plant six rifle bullets with water-spout effects. Then the fish sounded and hung to the bottom.

Just as always with a wounded animal about, up from somewhere came a troup of canni-bals—the ever-present, ever-prowling, sneaking

"IT TOOK CONSIDERABLE TACKLE TO DRAG HIM UP ONTO THE BEACH"

—*Page 207*

sharks; but our harpoons were all in use. The sharks were free to glide around at will. In due course of time the bullets had their telling effect and inch by inch we heaved and hauled and at last we had the monster at the surface. Another shot settled the contest, and with ropes and cables we made him fast to the stern and with "Hink's" boat up ahead, we towed our prize back to the shore.

It took considerable tackle and several pulleys to drag him up onto the beach but at last we had the fish in position and ready for the camera. It could only be an estimate, but we all concurred in setting him down at 2,000 pounds.

To give an idea of his size my little daughter stood on his back, held out her hand on one side to her good old Nanna and on the other side to Mrs. Hinkley, who in turn held out their hands to the Captain and Mr. Hinkley, both of whom stood on the end of a flipper. Thus were five people with arms outstretched standing crosswise on the back of that monster devil-fish.

My first experience in harpooning was with

the heavy, speedy whip-ray. I tell of this because it illustrates a point in which the actor has to play an important part.

Excitement was intense. "Now!" said the Captain, and I made my first throw, let everything go and jumped backward. I mustn't be caught in the rope and pulled overboard. But, alas, what was the result? The launch passed over the line and in a second it was wound around the propeller. Just then we spied a shark, but it was of no use, for we were obliged to spend the next half-hour in trying to free the snarl. I have since learned to "stand by" and "save" the line in case of a miss.

Let me repeat again, however, that while one should "stand by," one above all else should see that he is neither standing on, nor over, the line. In that fast uncoiling rope, it is very easy to be caught, which might indeed result seriously.

My next attempt was more successful. I made a true hit. Off "flew" the ray at an amazing speed. I grabbed the line, but this time I held on too hard and in a second the fast run-

"THUS WERE FIVE PEOPLE WITH ARMS OUTSTRETCHED STANDING CROSSWISE ON THE BACK OF THAT MONSTER DEVIL-FISH"

—Page 207

"MY FIRST EXPERIENCE WAS WITH THE HEAVY, SPEEDY
WHIP-RAY"

—*Page* 207

ning line had burned my hands like a hot poker. "I'll learn," I said to the Captain. And so I did. That night I was as proud as any boy with my first two trophies from the harpoon.

Of all my harpooning adventures, perhaps the one that stands out most vividly in my mind is my contest with a sawfish. For many years I had listened to stories of this huge strange fish, but it had never been my fortune to run across one.

It was on one beautiful afternoon when, with the ladies aboard the launch, we were running out over the shoals off Trestle No. 2, headed for the Gulf Stream. Always in the hope of seeing something new, especially when passing over a favorable shoal, one of us would be standing in the bow with harpoon in easy reach.

This time both the Captain and I were on watch.

"There he is!" said the Captain. "Sawfish dead ahead!"

The word was passed back and great excitement prevailed. My chance had come. Whose nerves wouldn't be set tingling? Who wouldn't be tense with excitement at such a moment? It was an adventure that I had sought for many years and now it was at hand.

I'll pass over the chase and skilful maneuvering for position, fraught with sharp quick orders and strained attention. I'll bring you to the psychological moment.

"Shoot!" said the Captain.

I trembled. I shot. I missed. I trembled. And still again I trembled.

"Speed her up!" shouted the Captain.

Again we were in position.

"Take aim. Be careful. Shoot!" he said.

Again I shot. Again I missed. Heavens! did I have stage fright or "buck fever"? Was I going to lose my chance of years? And all the while I could hear an excited, high-pitched voice from the stern crying, "Get him, Daddy! Get him, Daddy!"

The fish was running into deeper water. Soon my prey would be out of reach. "Quick or you'll lose him!" came a cold hard statement of fact. Again I shot and this time the harpoon went strong and fair. I hit my mark. Out went the line and the contest was on.

"THAT NIGHT I WAS AS PROUD AS ANY BOY WITH MY
FIRST TWO TROPHIES FROM THE HARPOON"

—*Page* 213

"TWO SAWFISH IN LESS THAN TWO HOURS"

—*Page* 219

It was a great old struggle. Little by little, we worked the sawfish to the boat. "Look out!" shouted the Captain, and at that moment a long, sharp-toothed saw swung high above the bow. We dodged back just in time. Again he swung —again we dodged. Woe be unto him who gets in the path of that powerful and dangerous weapon. We ended the fight with a few telling shots from a handy revolver and the trophy was ours. He measured thirteen feet ten inches, and had fifty teeth on his saw. That saw is now a treasured memento of this contest.

Hardly had we finished with that adventure when we spied another sawfish. This time the Captain handled the harpoon and gave us all a splendid exhibition of his skill. Two sawfish in less than two hours was indeed a record.

There is one more short tale of harpooning that I should like to add to these adventures. This was the hunt on Boot Key Shoal. I can picture the day now—the tide was right, the water was clear, there was hardly a breath of wind to ruffle the surface. I can see those little groups of barren islands fairly covered with lazy pelicans sunning themselves. I can see

Sombrero Light standing on guard at sea five miles away. I can see the gulls gracefully swooping down and stopping for perhaps a second to pick up some morsel floating on the water or dive beneath its surface to capture some tiny fish.

Slowly we worked out over these shoals—keen and watchful for those moving shadows which proclaim the ghostly prowlers of the sea. There were the shadows—there were the sharks. Never had I seen so many.

We began our attack on those tough-hided monsters, the nurse sharks. Many a time a toggle would hit true and clean and yet fail to penetrate far enough to get a secure hold. Later we turned our attention to the more vicious cannibals, the leopard sharks and the bluenose sharks.

When finally we "rang the bell" on the morning's work, we had what proved to be our record. There were in this catch five nurse sharks, one leopard shark, one bluenose shark, one sawfish, one whip-ray and two green turtles. Strenuous it was, but what a morning! It was well into the afternoon before we had our trophies

"I CAN SEE THOSE LITTLE GROUPS OF BARREN ISLANDS FAIRLY COVERED WITH LAZY PELICANS"

—Page 219

"A GREEN TURTLE"

—Page 220

properly hung for photographic purposes, but just before we pressed the button, one heavy monster broke loose and sank beneath the surface out of reach. Alas! our picture never can stand as a complete record of that morning's sport. But who cared, when the sea had been rid of seven sharks and the chef had transformed the turtles into "viands for a king."

The sun had set—the sky was brilliant in its canopy of color—the tarpon were waiting for us at the trestles, and from the fishing launches lazily bumping at the stern we heard the cheerful signal from the Captain, "Let's go."

CHAPTER VIII

NO one cruising along the Florida Keys can fail to be interested in that marvelous construction of engineering skill, the Florida East Coast Railway. Even one entirely devoid of any technical or engineering interest is singularly impressed with what has been accomplished. It takes but small imagination indeed to wonder how Henry M. Flagler, Florida's greatest builder and developer, could have in his seventy-sixth year conceived the idea of constructing a railroad from the mainland of Florida, across the Florida Keys, to the island and city of Key West, and then be bold enough to carry his plan into effect. We who are conversant with the tides, the winds, the constantly changing sand bars; we who have seen mile after mile of massive concrete arches and pillars of reenforced concrete coming up out of the ocean from solid bed-rock, not only appreciate but admire the

"STRENUOUS IT WAS—BUT WHAT A MORNING!"

—*Page* 220

courage and ability of that great constructive American, and we are indeed gratified that Mr. Flagler lived to see the dream of many years an accomplished fact.

From the mainland to Key West, a distance of approximately one hundred and seven miles, is this string of small islands known as the Florida Keys ("key" being a corruption from the Spanish "cayo" meaning "island"), with channels between varying in depth from a few inches at low tide to twenty feet. Through these channels the waters of the Gulf of Mexico run into the Atlantic Ocean and back again with each tide. The flow of the tide through these channels and over these shoals is singularly varying, affected largely by the wind. It is a common occurrence to have the tide on the ocean side rising while the tide on the gulf side is still running out under the trestles. Sometimes the tide runs in one direction at a greater or lesser speed for a period of eighteen hours.

This construction was commenced in 1905; and very interesting records, issued by the Chamber of Commerce of Key West, Florida, show that when this work was begun there were no precedents for much of the work, and numerous problems were encountered that rail-road builders had never before been obliged to overcome. Where the water between these keys was shallow, the construction was easy and re-quired only the throwing up by steam shovels of the marl and limestone rock adjacent to the line of proposed embankment. In other places where the water was deep and the flow of the current strong, the problem was met by solid concrete piers of huge size and solid concrete arches. Many a time have I looked up in awe from below at those immense arches of concrete and those spans of steel. Many a time have I glided under one of the arches at the east-ward end of Knight's Key Trestle and tried in vain to see the farther end lost in the horizon seven miles away.

The construction of the road-bed presented a variety of problems hardly equaled, as far as I know, by similar work anywhere else. The building of the road-bed south from Homestead was through the swamps of the Everglades. The land was low and partially covered with water. Records show that it could not be graded with any appliances ever used for such purposes. Emergency dredges were constructed that would float in shallow water and these were started southward, each eating out a channel for itself and discharging the material on what became the road-bed.

The material was marl or coral rock which is found in a thick plastic mass, dazzling white in color, which by exposure to air and sun becomes harder and harder as time goes by. To-day a canal from twenty to thirty feet wide borders the road on either side for many miles before it reaches the keys.

Any one exploring these keys can appreciate the dense jungles of vegetation which had to be penetrated, but this was largely a matter of perseverance and unusual hardship. It was, of course, when open water was reached that some of the most serious problems and difficulties were encountered.

Three great viaducts spanning wide gaps of water between the keys are typical of all. The Long Key Bridge, 2¾ miles in length built on arched spans, is perhaps the most picturesque. These arches, each about forty feet long, records show were built on trap rock brought from Clinton on the Hudson River and set in heavily reenforced concrete. The railroad company reports that this bridge was among the most expensive pieces of work on the entire line, costing at that time approximately $500,000 per mile.

Knight's Key Bridge, stretching a little more than seven miles, is carried five miles on 80-foot deck plate steel girders laid on reenforced concrete piers, and two miles on concrete arches.

The Bahia Honda Bridge is 5,056 feet long. It is of the "through truss" type in which the trusses rise many feet above the track level and flank the moving train. In this bridge are thirteen spans, each 128 feet 6 inches long; thirteen spans each 186 feet long; one span, which we fishermen call the center arch, is 247 feet 6 inches long; and then there are nine spans of deck plate steel girders each eighty feet. The deepest water in the construction work was found here—approximately thirty feet to bed-rock.

Three drawbridges are placed at intervals.

One at Jew-fish Creek, one at Trestle No. 5, and one at Knight's Key Bridge just below Pidgeon Key, called Moser Channel Draw.

There are still many evidences of the tremendous amount of auxiliary construction that was necessary to complete this work. For instance, the old piles and wooden trestle work of many of the old temporary bridges are still in existence. There are evidences of old wharves, constructed hundreds of yards out into some deep channel. There are miles and miles of old wooden trestle work, notably around Marathon and Bahia Honda which were built out onto the marl flats where the necessary filling was obtained for many of the high embankments. Marathon, once the most important construction center, has to-day practically disappeared in abandoned neglect.

The first train was operated into Key West on January 22, 1912. Exact figures covering the cost of construction are unobtainable, but the closest estimate reached is forty-nine million dollars. It is interesting to note some of the hardships that were faced by those pioneers in road building. The original engineering plan contemplated six miles of open water spanned by bridges of concrete or steel. Owing to the actual and varying ebb and flow of the ocean tides, it was found that this was insufficient space and that eighteen miles of open water instead of six had to be provided.

The question of labor was one of the most perplexing. Between three and four thousand men were employed on the work for many months at a time. Many of these men were recruited through agencies in New York and Philadelphia. Twenty per cent. of the army of workmen on the keys were furnished by what was found to be a very efficient class of labor, the Spaniard, brought over from Cuba. The matter of water for drinking and domestic purposes was one of the first and most important problems to be solved. Borings were made in many places, as deep as two thousand feet through the limestone and coral rock to find an adequate supply of water, but without satisfying results. Then, as to-day, the entire water supply, outside of collected rain water, is brought in large tank cars from drilled wells near Homestead. Even the city of Key West itself to-day secures its water in just this way.

The matter of operating trains in safety over much of the exposed extension has been carefully worked out. The possibility of storms must make extra hazardous the operation of trains exposed to their fury. The viaducts have been built of stone and steel to withstand storm pressure four hundred per cent. greater than has ever been recorded in this latitude—in the hurricane of 1909, the wind reached a velocity of 125 miles an hour, and did serious and extensive damage to work under construction. One of the precautions for safety is that no train is permitted to run over the trestles at a speed greater than fifteen miles an hour. The constructing engineers, however, have declared that the strength of these great viaducts would warrant a speed of seventy miles an hour.

And so, from first to last, one looks with wonder and amazement at this great achievement—a living testimonial and monument for ages to come to the courage and ability of a great American.

CHAPTER IX

THE following facts and observations together with opinions and data concerning time, bait and tackle have been gathered not alone through my own observations and experiences, but from observations and experiences of my friend and "chief counselor," Captain Walter A. Starck, of Miami, Florida.

Captain Starck has spent many years of careful and intelligent study of fish and fishing along the Florida Keys, the West Coast and off the Island of Bemini. In fact, there is hardly a month for many years that he has not devoted a substantial part of his time to just this kind of life and study. It is to him that I owe the success of my adventures with rod and harpoon. He has been ever courteous, ever considerate and ever helpful. For the active fisherman, he is ever ready. He is one of those who appreciate the value of time and utilize it to extraordinary advantage, which almost without exception means that he is ever ready with the *proper bait* to be used *at the proper time.* The tide is never wrong. The day is never too hot or too cold. The conditions are never so bad that he has not something to suggest or some place to go. He is tireless in his efforts. He is contented to have his fishermen save their fish for photographic purposes or when such fish can be used. On the other hand, he is a careful and intelligent sportsman, cooperating with the fishermen in their endeavors to free such fish as cannot be utilized. At all times, he uses rare judgment in matters of fishing and navigation. I am always grateful to him for any opinion that he is willing to give on any matter pertaining to fish or fishing.

TARPON

Seasons. Undoubtedly the best time for tarpon fishing is during the months of May, June and July. Many people not conversant with the climate of Florida naturally think that the heat at that time of year is insufferable. It is quite the contrary along the Florida Keys. It is true that there are times in the middle of the day when one could without question call it extremely hot, but never have I experienced such extreme heat as often is visited upon Washington, New York, Boston, or the West. There is usually a breeze during the day, while the nights are invariably cool and comfortable. One never experiences stifling heat.

Rarely are tarpon taken in January. Occasionally they are taken in February. Frequently they are taken in March, but this depends considerably on the varying weather. With a continuance of east winds in March, one is almost sure to hook a tarpon. One is reasonably sure to get good tarpon fishing in April. In the months of May, June and July, all the places I have described in Chapter III should yield many good fish, especially the noted channels of Bahia Honda. Here we have taken as many as fifteen splendid fish in one evening. Again I am prompted to speak of the importance of fresh bait. On this particular evening the fish were all over the bay and striking well. There was another party fishing there, and as far as I know they never jumped a fish. We had fresh bait; they didn't. Curiously enough, however, in the months of February and March, Bahia Honda is less favorable. Undoubtedly this is due to the fact that the feed is more plentiful in the shallow channels, and such places as Grouper Channel, Knight's Key, Tom's Harbor and Trestle No. 5, will undoubtedly produce more fish.

As a rule, the first places of the season to yield fish are Grouper Channel and Tom's Harbor. Grouper Channel will produce the larger fish, while Tom's Harbor the smaller fish.

I have already stated that as early as the month of March our party had taken as high as sixty-five tarpon. At any season and especially in the earlier months a most favorable time is at the end of a few days' easterly blow with the prospects of a change of wind and a coming storm from the west or north. At such a time, one is almost sure to find the fish active and ready to strike.

Time of Day. The best time of day is just

before sunset and from then on into the night. I have had many evidences and have described certain instances which clearly indicate that dark nights are very much better than moon-light nights. And on clear nights, one should plan, if possible, to fish just before the moon has come up or just after the moon has gone down. Very often early morning fishing is pro-ductive of good results and fishing is frequently good up to noon. The poorest time to fish is between noon and five o'clock in the afternoon.

Regardless of time or condition, it is very rarely that any fish are taken at slack tide. Occasionally, however, a tarpon will take a live mullet at such a time.

Fishing Grounds. The following is a list of the tarpon grounds from Biscayne Bay south:

Barnes' Sound, preferably along the west shore
Tavernier Creek, near the railroad arch (baby tarpon)
Lignum Vitæ Channel
Trestle No. 2 and channels
Trestle No. 5 and channels

Westward end of Long Key Trestle (eastward side of the two aprons)

The two Tom's Harbor Trestles (medium fish as a rule)

Key Vaca Channel

Knight's Key Trestle and channels

Sister Creek

Grouper Channel

Trestles between Grouper Channel and Bahia Honda (baby tarpon)

Bahia Honda Trestle, channels and bay

There are also several channels well out in Fonda Bay which at times yield fish.

Tackle. The true sportsman is always desirous of using as light tackle as possible. This means two things—the exercising of greater skill on the part of the fisherman and greater freedom of play on the part of the fish. One should, however, select the proper tackle with intelligent consideration of the character of grounds he intends to fish.

For instance, in such places as Knight's Key Trestle, where one has to contend against strong tide, concrete piers, and sunken piles, the heavier tackle should be used. Often one has to exert considerable strain to save one's fish from fouling against pier or pile, which maneuvers are complicated by strong tide, and under such conditions, the heavy tackle is most necessary. It has always seemed to me absurd and rather a matter of false sportsmanship, and almost a matter of "posing," to use such light tackle as will prevent the fisherman from exercising reasonable control over a fish maneuvering in a dangerous place. Unnecessarily broken and fouled lines are always to me regrettable situations, and do more harm to the fish than a careful and successful "taking" with subsequent release.

Rods. What I consider to be a reasonable size for heavy rods is:

> Tip length: 5⅓ feet
> Weight: 12 to 15 ounces
> Butt length: 20 inches

Personally, I am against the agate tip. It is easily cracked or broken, which means rough or sharp edges, causing cut lines.

Where agate tips are used, they should be

subject to careful and constant inspection. One of the common ways of damaging the tip is from carelessness in reeling in the line so far and so fast that the metal swivel attached to the leader is snapped against the agate. This carelessness occurs particularly when one is reeling in at night and cannot readily see what progress he is making. It is a common fault of the beginner, in his haste to reel in, not to stop reeling until he feels the swivel bring up fast against the tip.

Reels holding from 200 to 300 yards of line are necessary.

Lines. What I consider to be a reasonable range of "heavy" lines is from Nos. 24 to 30. It is my opinion that when one can safely use a lighter line, one can safely use a lighter rod. To those who are not conversant with the meaning of the numbers, I venture to explain, that a No. 24 means that the line is twisted with twenty-four strands; a No. 27 means that the line is twisted with twenty-seven strands, etc.

As there is so much "severe water" in so many places along the keys, I have preferred the No. 27 line for usual heavy work.

It must also be borne in mind that there is always greater strain on the tackle when fishing from a launch.

Now, in some of the channels, such as the channel of Key Vaca, one can and should use "light tackle." This ordinarily means sailfish tackle (see the description under *Sailfish* in this chapter).

It should be noted, however, that while the range of lines for sailfish is from No. 9 to No. 18, it would be unwise on heavy tarpon to use anything smaller than No. 15. I should recommend No. 18 line, although at Key Vaca one evening I was fortunate in landing on a No. 15 line two big fish, one weighing 160 pounds, and one weighing 175 pounds.

It is a necessary precaution on the part of a salmon fisherman each night to dry out his line. This is not necessary, however, in this Florida fishing, when you are using your tackle every day. In fact, we have found that it is harmful to wet and dry out a line completely every day. The strength of one's tackle is of paramount importance, and no chances should be taken with old or questionable lines. One's whole outfit should be continually under the most careful inspection. As a suggestion, after a line has been given quite some use, it is a good plan to change it on the reel, end for end. It is when you have jumped a prize fish that you want to be sure that, as far as the tackle is concerned, there can be no question as to its strength.

Oftentimes a person will thoughtlessly hang up his rod with the hook caught loosely on the bar of the reel. This is a natural error, but it often results in serious consequences. The hook is apt to touch the line, and in a short time leave a spot of rust. The action of the rust weakens the line.

Leaders. For leaders, one uses what is known as piano wire, size 9 or 10. This is purchased in one roll, and can be cut at desired lengths, which for ordinary purposes are about eight feet. The leader is attached to a swivel, which in turn is attached to the line. When one is through fishing, the hook and leader should be taken off the line. This prevents any part of the leader or hook, which rusts easily, from coming in contact with the line.

After landing a fish, be sure there are no

kinks in the leader. If the leader is considerably twisted, the twist should be cut off, or a new leader used, as it is always dangerous to use a leader that is not in perfect condition.

Hooks. We have always had our best success on a 9/10 tarpon hook. When "cut bait" is used, one should attach the leader to the hook in such a way as to leave the end of the leader protruding about two inches. This protruding end, called the "hairpin," is caught through the "head" of the bait, while the hook is pressed

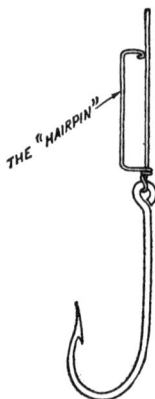

THE "HAIRPIN"

through the "body" of the bait. This allows the bait to troll straight through the water, and leaves the hook well back in the body. The illustration gives an idea of the above suggestion.

You will notice the "little loop" on the extreme end of the leader. When the bait is adjusted, that "little loop" is sprung back and caught around the main body of the leader. (See description of preparing tarpon bait on page 258.)

An expert captain will often take a tarpon into the boat by passing a rope through the mouth and out through the gills without the aid of a gaff, but this requires most careful and delicate handling. The gaff is the surest means of ending a successful catch. The gaff should not be used, however, when the fish is to be released. Perhaps the easiest way to free a fish is to hold the leader taut in your hand, and by lifting his head just above the surface of the water, the tarpon will usually shake out the hook.

A point well worth remembering is to ease off somewhat the tension drag on your reel (the little wheel right under the handle) as you bring your fish to the boat. With a fish on a short line near the boat and a hard-set tension drag, any quick sharp movement on the part of the fish is apt to tear the hook out. When the captain has the fish on the gaff, the fisherman should release both set drags, allowing the reel to run free, otherwise tackle is often broken by a fish suddenly tearing away from the gaff. One should be ready, however, to use the thumb break to prevent slack line or the reel over-running.

Fishing Belts. These leather belts are necessary supports for the rod while handling any big fish. (See illustration, " 'Hink' in action" on page 249.)

SAILFISH

Seasons. I consider January, February and March to be the best months for sailfishing.

My experience over several years has been that the best fishing reaches its climax just about two or three days before the full of the moon in March, and from then on it declines with intermittent success in April and May.

Mr. Fred C. N. Parke, of Long Key, Florida, a very keen student of the sailfish, writes me, "They are a peculiar fish and something about

" 'HINK' IN ACTION"

—*Page* 248

which we know but little. They are on the coast all the year and I presume they spawn there, for they have been taken as small as three pounds." Incidentally, very considerable credit is due Mr. Parke for his taxidermy work displayed in the mounted fish which decorate the main hall of the Long Key Fishing Camps.

Time of Day. As to the time of day, we have always had our best luck from the morning's start up to about noon, and then from two o'clock until sunset. . A good breeze is always better than a calm day, and clear water is most desirable.

Fishing Grounds. While sailfish are taken all along the coast, on the edge of the Gulf Stream, as far north as Cape Canaveral, I have always had my best luck on the following grounds:

Off Tavernier Creek (Work N. E. and S. W. from Conch Reef)

Off Trestle No. 2 (Work off Alligator Light S. W. to off Tennessee Buoy)

Off Moser Channel (Work N. E. from off Moser Channel Buoy to off Sombrero Light)

The grounds off Trestle No. 2 are easily reached from the Long Key Fishing Camps.

Rods. What I consider to be a reasonable size for light rods, for use on sailfish, reef fish, and tarpon (to be taken in still or free water) is:

> Tip length: about 62 inches
> Weight: 6 to 8 ounces
> Butt length: 14 inches

As this tackle is used for the most part in open water, the range of lines depends largely upon the fancy of the fisherman. This range is from No. 9 to No. 18. No. 9 is, however, so light that the greatest care and skill must be exercised. As stated before, when sailfish tackle is used for tarpon, nothing smaller than No. 15 line should be considered. No. 12 line I have always found to be a good average weight for sailfish. Reels holding from 200 to 300 yards of line are necessary.

Leaders. For leader, No. 8 wire is preferable. This is to be attached to the line with a swivel.

Hooks. When whole fish are used for bait, such as a whole balao, two hooks are preferable. The hook attached to the line is smaller than the second hook, and is ordinarily about size 8/o. A swivel is attached to the eye of the second hook, which is ordinarily about size 9/o. The free eye of the swivel is slipped over the barb of the first hook, and so pressed that it cannot slip off. The first hook, attached to the leader, is caught to the "head" of the bait, while the second hook is pressed into the body. (See description of preparing sailfish bait, page 263.)

The same cautions in handling line and reel suggested in tarpon fishing are equally applicable to sailfishing.

BONEFISH

Seasons. The bonefish feed on the banks at all seasons of the year, but these fish as a rule take better in the warmer months.

Fishing Grounds.

Banks off Rodriguez Key
Banks around Trestle No. 2.

Banks around Tom's Harbor Trestle
Banks at Key Vaca Channel
Banks off Boot Key
Along many of the beaches

Rods. A five- or six-foot one, or two-piece
bait casting rod of perhaps 4½ to 6 ounces, with
large free guides, is the best type to use.

Lines. A No. 6 line on a free-running reel,
holding about 300 yards, is necessary.

Hooks. Two No. 3/o or 4/o hooks can be
used where the shoals are reasonably free of
coral or other obstructions; otherwise it is safer
to use one hook. The reason for this is a running fish is apt to pick up some obstruction
with the second free hook. The reason for two
hooks is that small fish, spoken of as nibblers or
crabs, often steal the bait off of one or the other
hook, making it obvious that two hooks baited
are better than one. However, as stated above,
it is dangerous to use two hooks on rough bottom. These hooks, a short distance apart,
should be so attached to the line as to leave a
double end or loop about eight inches long.
Attached to the end of the loop is a sinker suffi-

ciently heavy to give weight and carry to a cast. Some fishermen believe that a gut hook is necessary. Personally, I believe a plain eye hook is better, the light line being more flexible than a stiffer gut. This may be merely a notion on my part, however; yet I have seen both types of hooks used in the same boat at the same time, with better results from the plain hook.

The importance and skill in casting for bonefish is comparable to the importance and skill for hooking a sailfish. One should have a perfectly free running reel and as a suggestion, before the first cast is made, it is well to pull out and wet fifty or sixty feet of line, the result being that the line will unwind with greater freedom, insuring a smooth and successful cast.

REEF FISH TACKLE

The same tackle used for sailfish is equally practical for all the great variety of reef fish. Here, however, you should use a single hook, about size No. 9. In trolling for Spanish mackerel, one should use a No. 4/0 hook.

BAIT

The importance of the right bait at the right time cannot be overestimated. We have made a most careful study of this subject and have watched where, how, and under what conditions it has failed or has been successful.

It is commonly known that in the height of the season, the mullet is the "best bet" for tarpon.

Right here let me cite an instance that gave us food for thought. Our party was down for ten days' fishing. It was the last of May. When we arrived, there was another party of four already on the ground. They fished with reasonable constancy; they were still in the neighborhood when we left; but in those ten days they never took a tarpon. In those ten days' fishing we took thirty-five splendid fish.

Now that sounds like bragging, but let me assure you that in no way do I lay those results to any possible skill in handling or playing the fish, nor to any "wise" knowledge of "just the spot" to fish over.

I lay it to one thing, and that is *bait*. At that

time, for some reason, it was extremely difficult to secure fresh bait. Never did our captain ask us to use bait that had been kept over and put on ice several days, thereby becoming soft and perhaps somewhat "strong." Never did he ask us to use "salted" bait, which is always the easiest way out.

To secure fresh bait meant taking the launches and cruising off for many miles, being gone many hours, and putting in the hardest kind of physical work. It requires, as a matter of fact, considerable strength as well as skill to throw those umbrella-like nets. Many a time a cast is made with no results. I do not hesitate to say that after a morning's hard fishing, it takes considerable moral determination and physical energy for the captain to start right out after luncheon, in the heat of the day, and work for three or four hours, casting a heavy net. How easy it is to say, "Well, we've got plenty of bait on ice that we netted three days ago" or "We have a good supply aboard of salted mullet."

And so I deny any spirit of "braggadocio" when I tell of our results as compared to the results of our neighbors. I claim that we had the right kind of bait, which was *fresh*. I have had practically that same experience with the sailfish; therefore, I cannot emphasize too strongly the importance of fresh bait.

Tarpon Bait. The best all-round bait for tarpon is the mullet. When a whole mullet is used, which must be of medium size, it is necessary to cut out the backbone and dorsal fin, otherwise the bait is too stiff and revolves or sheers about when dragged through the water. The hook is pressed through the lips. This bait is acceptable at times when a cut bait does not attract. Cut bait, as a rule, however, is the best of all the tarpon lures. A large-sized mullet is preferable, and it should be prepared with great care. Cut off the head, just forward of the pectoral and ventral fins. Scrape off the scales, and cut open the belly its full length. Then lay the fish on a flat board and, pressing down firmly with the left hand, slice the fish lengthwise in half just above the backbone. By using care, and a sharp knife, one can slice the tail in half. The result is two complete sides, each having a tail. One side still has the backbone, which should be sliced off, leaving both

"I CLAIM THAT WE HAD THE RIGHT KIND OF BAIT, WHICH WAS FRESH"

—*Page 257*

sides exactly alike. The flabby part of the belly and ventral fin should be cut away, and the head of the bait should be rounded off so as to bring the head to a blunt point, as shown in the illustration. The loose end of the wire,

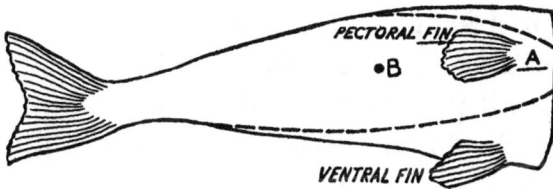

or "hairpin," is pressed through a little slit in the head marked *A* which has previously been made when preparing the bait. The loop on the end of the "hairpin" is simply caught around the leader. (See illustration on page 246.) The hook is then pressed through the body of the bait at such a spot, marked *B,* as will allow a direct pull on the hook, the idea being to have the hook well back and reasonably concealed against the body of the bait. The loose wire end or "hairpin" is thus necessary to hold up the head of the bait, in order that the bait will pull straight, giving a natural appearance to the movement of the lure.

Let me caution the beginner again to strike back hard and quick the instant a tarpon takes the bait. Often the heavy strike of a tarpon gives to the fisherman the impression that the fisherman himself has done the striking, with the result that the tarpon throws the hook on the first jump. The inside of a tarpon's mouth is of smooth, almost shell-like hardness, which means that to set the hook properly, the fisherman should set back with a quick, decisive stroke.

When using the live bait, one should select a medium-sized mullet, and hook it through the lips. With careful handling, the mullet will keep alive for quite some time. As stated before, give the tarpon plenty of time to take the live bait before striking. The live mullet is the best bait on a slack tide.

There are times, especially in the earlier part of the season, when a whole balao is the favorite bait. In preparing this bait, break off the beak of the balao, take out the backbone, and hook through the head. The larger size balaos for tarpon bait are preferable.

Occasionally, a No. 6 plain silver, one hook spoon will raise a fish, but this is only tried, as a rule, when the mullet or balao fail to attract. It is hard to get a successful set with a spoon; consequently it is easy for the tarpon to "throw" the hook.

In trolling for tarpon, one should have the launch throttled down to as slow a speed as possible, making but little headway against the tide—just enough to change from arch to arch, or from spot to spot; but, as stated in a previous chapter, fishing from a rowboat is preferable whenever possible.

Sailfish Bait. The medium-sized balao we have found to be the best bait for sailfish. This should be prepared the same as described for tarpon. When two hooks are used (see description of hooks) one presses the top, or smaller hook, down through the head, the second hook through the belly from the inside—the body of the hook being substituted, as it were, for the backbone, which has been taken out. We have also used, with good success, half a medium-sized needle-fish, prepared as one prepares a mullet for cut bait. A strip of mackerel belly, about six inches long, tapered to resemble the shape of a balao, is often acceptable.

A bronzed and silvered wooden whirler, or plug, about eight inches long, one inch diameter at one end and tapered off at the other end, is attached with swivel to a short line of about fifteen or twenty feet, and dragged at the stern. This revolves in the water and is supposed to help attract the fish. Many times have I seen sailfish swim right up and tap the plug before we could pull it away; in fact, several times, I have seen them tear it loose. This proves that a sailfish will strike at a bait very close to the boat. Many people make the rather natural mistake of fishing with too long a line. This prevents the fisherman from seeing the fish approach, and gives him no opportunity to tempt by one trick or another an indifferent fish to take the bait. Trolling with about sixty-five or seventy feet of line, under ordinary conditions, is quite sufficient and in the long run will bring better results.

In the early days of fishing, it was considered best to troll at a slow rate of speed, but to-day it has been proved that sailfish will attack the bait with more determination if the launch is going at least six to eight miles an hour. Often an indifferent fish will take the bait by increasing the speed—rarely by decreasing the speed.

Bonefish Bait. Hermit crabs are the best bait. Care should be used in breaking the shells not to smash the crab. Break off the claws. Press the hook through the head or hard part of the crab, allowing the barb to be hidden in the soft part of the body. Small white sand crabs are possible bait, as well as quahogs, but nothing is as satisfactory as the hermit crab.

Reef Fish Bait. Sailfish bait is practical for all the reef fish, with the exception of the amber-jack.

A speed of six to seven miles an hour is best for wahoo, kingfish, barracuda, and cero mackerel. A speed of three to four miles an hour is best for grouper.

While amber-jack will often take while trolling, one can get the best results by using live bait, such as grunts or porgies, hooked through the back. By drifting around, one can readily locate the amber-jack, and when a fish is hooked, he will tole up many more of his friends, thus furnishing the fisherman with keen, exhilarating sport.

For Spanish mackerel, a small strip of fish belly about four inches long is the best bait. These delectable fish are found in the channels and around the trestles. One should troll at a speed of about six miles an hour.

Bottom Fish. These little fish, such as grunts, porgies, etc., are found in the channels and around "rock beds." Fresh crawfish is the best bait, but very good success can be had with salted crawfish.

Securing Bait. Mullet are found in schools in protected places close to the shore, and are caught by casting over the school a weighted net which opens up like an umbrella. This is called a cast net. It is not only very hard and quick work to throw this net, but it takes considerable skill as well.

The best time to net mullet is at high tide when they are feeding in the shoal places. Schools of these fish are readily seen on a bright clear day.

A dark night is the best time to get balaos.

"CASTING THAT HEAVY NET"

"IT REQUIRES, AS A MATTER OF FACT, CONSIDERABLE STRENGTH AS WELL AS SKILL TO THROW OUT THOSE UMBRELLA-LIKE NETS"

These fish can be found oftentimes in the channels as well as on the shoals. A lamp placed in the bow of a rowboat clearly discloses these little fish swimming about the surface. They can readily be caught in a long-handled dip-net. They can also be caught during the daytime on hook and line. One should anchor a row-boat on the edge of a channel. Attach a cork stopper about two feet above the hook and let it float with the tide. A bit of crawfish is good bait.

Crawfish are taken with a two- or five-prong spear, and are found around rock heads.

Hermit crabs are found by wading close to the shore, especially in such places where the mangrove bushes grow out into the water. A piece of dead fish in the water will often attract these crabs.

As I began this chapter, so will I end it, emphasizing the importance of *fresh* bait—*first, last,* and *always.*

AFTERWORD

If this book has given pleasure to him or to her who has instinctive love of nature's sport— if this book, perchance, has given to the veteran fisherman some helpful thought or some new angle—if this book has tempted a stranger sportsman to enter this enchanted land and share in the joys of beauty and in the thrills of sport, then am I indeed happy, for I will know that the tale of my adventures with Rod and Harpoon has not been written in vain.